MW00570559

The Canadian's Guide to Debt-Free Living

WILEY

The Canadian's Guide to Debt-Free Living

by Andrew Dagys, CPA, CMA, and
Mary Reed

WILEY

Publisher's Acknowledgments

Authors: Andrew Dagys, CPA, CMA, and Mary Reed

Senior Acquisitions Editor: Tracy Boggier

Project Manager: Susan Pink

Compilation Editor: Georgette Beatty

Production Editor: Siddique Shaik

Cover Design: Wiley

Cover Images: © puruan / Getty Images, © stockish / Shutterstock

The Canadian's Guide to Debt-Free Living

Published by John Wiley & Sons, Inc.
111 River St.
Hoboken, NJ 07030-5774
http://www.wiley.com

For general information on our other products and services, please contact our Business Development Department in the U.S. at 317-572-3205.

Library of Congress Control Number: 2019942823

ISBN 978-1-119-60933-9 (pbk)

Manufactured in the United States of America

V10011105_061219

Table of Contents

1

Getting into Debt

Knowing the different types of debts and expenses that drain the money out of your pocket every month can help you prioritize your payments and identify places to cut back. This knowledge also helps you assess how effective your choices are likely to be; some of the available options may or may not help, depending on the type of debt you have.

Debts versus Expenses

Debt is anything you owe. Debt can be very short term, like ordering a meal in a restaurant and having to pay for it before you leave, or long term, like buying a house with a 30-year mortgage. Whatever you have to pay is a debt. But to understand debt's impact on your financial future, you need to understand credit.

Personal credit has two aspects: having funds put at your disposal (loan, cash advance) and time given for payment of goods and services sold on trust (credit cards, instalment plans). Both involve your written, contracted promise of future repayment, almost always with interest.

Credit

The way you get credit is by establishing creditworthiness, which is a measure of your reliability to repay a loan. Lenders consider three factors in determining creditworthiness:

- **Capacity:** The measure of your ability to repay; refers primarily to your income and the duration of your employment.
- **Capital:** The value of what you own, including property, vehicles, investments, and savings.
- **Character:** Generally regarded as the most important factor. To determine this, lenders rely only on reports of your credit history.

Credit bureaus collect information on the borrowing and repayment patterns of all consumers. They put everything about you that may affect repayment — such as the name of your employer, income, mortgage, outstanding bills, legal problems, available credit — into this history. Credit reports that are sent to potential lenders, and which can be requested by employers when you apply for jobs, are based on your credit history.

The reason why credit histories suffer so badly when you don't pay your bills is that credit is not merely a convenience, it is a legal contract built on a foundation of trust. In failing to pay bills, you are both breaking the law and betraying trust. Most consumers don't think of credit this way — but creditors do. You may want to think about how you view credit, because it really affects how you use it.

You can research your credit history on your own. You can purchase a copy of your up-to-date credit history from companies such as Equifax (www.equifax.ca) — the same resource creditors use to evaluate your credit history.

What are the pros and cons of credit?

Securing credit is applying for a loan: You ask a financial institution to lend, or "rent," you the use of its money. For the use of the money, you can expect to pay extra money. The terms of your agreement specify the rate of interest — the extra money you pay to repay your debt to the institution that issued the loan.

The benefits of establishing credit are significant. They include the following:

- The ability to make a major purchase when you don't have immediate cash for the item
- A sense of security realizing that you can handle an unexpected emergency by using credit
- The convenience of shopping without carrying a lot of cash
- Monthly itemized credit statements that enable you to track your purchases
- Worldwide acceptance

Establishing credit is a double-edged sword. With its benefits come some major disadvantages, including the following:

- Easily available credit can easily make spending second nature.
- If you can't pay off your credit balances on time, you hurt your credit rating.
- You can fall into the trap of paying off only some of the credit debt instead of paying the entire amount when it is due.
- When you add credit expenses to the stated price, you end up paying more than you expected. Sometimes you pay more than double!

For many Canadians, an over-aggressive use of available credit can result in a debt load that is difficult to sustain.

Is there an acceptable level of credit?

When credit card offers start coming, you'll notice that they seem to compete with each other by raising the level of credit they will extend to you. You may get a small thrill when you receive a letter from a credit card company telling you that you're prequalified for a line of credit that boggles your mind.

These days, companies are offering $10,000, $25,000, and even up to $100,000 lines of credit. This is absurd! Why would anyone want that much credit card debt? You may be flattered to think that someone would extend you a line of credit for large amounts of money, and you may be tempted to say, "You never know when that money would come in handy." Don't give in to temptation — you need to think seriously about the level of credit debt your income can tolerate. Just because a lender is willing to extend that line of credit doesn't mean you have to use it. Still, the temptation to do so is great, and many fall into the trap of using their line of credit to the maximum.

Imagine Mr. and Mrs. Conservative — the couple who pay cash for everything and don't owe anyone money. Their debts are paid. Their cars and house are paid for. Their children went to university and are now buying houses of their own. Yes, they borrowed money, but only to buy their home, and then they paid off the mortgage ahead of time. These two certainly weren't victims of the recent North American credit crisis, spawned by cheap interest rates on mortgages that had no business being written!

Now, imagine Mr. and Mrs. Bigspender — the couple you like to be with because they always pick up the tab for dinner. They talk about the expensive vacations they take and the fancy cars they drive. They live in a large home and have a cottage. They're up to their eyeballs in debt. They have no clue about how to change their spending and debt habits. Who's really having all the fun?

Your own comfort with credit card debt is likely to be somewhere in the middle. The following tables can help you figure out what your level of debt should be.

First, use Table 1-1 to identify the amount of debt you currently carry. The first two lines of the table are examples; fill in your own debts in the remaining lines. (Feel free to add lines if you need to.)

Creditor's Name	Loan	Total Due	Monthly	Maturity Payment
Main St. Bank	Car	$5,040	$140	36 months
Visa		$1,000	$120	10 months
Total debt				
Total monthly payments				

Table 1-1: *Monitoring Your Debts and Monthly Payments*

Most financial advisers recommend a personal debt limit of between 10 and 20 percent of your net income, maximum. To figure out your personal debt ratio, use Table 1-2.

Your monthly net income	
To accommodate debt of 20 percent, divide your net income by 5.	
To accommodate debt of 15 percent, divide your net income by 6.7.	
To accommodate debt of 10 percent, divide your net income by 10.	
Your monthly debt obligations (see the "Total monthly payments" line in Table 1-1)	
Calculate your debt margin (the ratio of debt to net income) by subtracting your monthly debt obligations from whichever level of debt you're comfortable with.	
Figure out your personal debt ratio by dividing your monthly debt obligations by your monthly net income.	

Table 1-2: *Determining Your Debt Ratio*

Table 1-2 applies simple math to help you determine the level of credit that's acceptable to you with your net income. If your debt margin is too close for comfort, sit down right now and write down three ways you can reduce your monthly credit-instalment payments. If your debt margin is comfortably less than your monthly credit obligations, don't rush out to buy things on credit. Instead, congratulate yourself on your frugality and revisit your savings plan.

What is the cost of credit?

Credit costs you money. For example, if you use your credit card to buy a $120 watch as a Christmas gift, here's how the costs add up: First, add in the provincial sales tax (PST) and goods and services tax (GST) (some provinces have a harmonized sales tax — HST). Then add in the finance charge. This charge, in its common usage, means the interest the credit company adds to single or cumulative transactions. If your finance charge is 19.2 percent and you pay $10 a month for a year to pay for the watch, your watch costs $120, plus PST and GST (or HST), plus about $15 in credit charges. All of a sudden, that watch seems a lot more expensive.

If you leave part of your bill unpaid, the creditor will charge you interest. The entire finance charge is taken from your payment, and your debt is reduced only by what's left over. For example, if you make a partial payment of $50 and the finance charge is $10, your debt is reduced not by $50 but by $40. Partial payments reduce your debt very slowly.

The more you buy on credit, the more you pay to reduce your debt. You know you're in credit trouble if you recognize any of the following warning signs:

- You find yourself charging more and more and paying with cash less and less.
- You let some bills slide and postpone payment for a month.

- You make partial payments instead of paying the entire bill.

- Your debt-to-net-income ratio exceeds 20 percent.

- You take out new credit cards to cover additional purchases after you max out the cards you're currently using.

 Only you can control what you buy on credit. Credit cards that get out of control cost you money and delay your ability to invest in your financial future. Try the following tips to reduce your credit costs:

- Shop for a low-cost or free credit card.

- Don't pay extra annual fees for premier cards that offer gold or platinum benefits unless you really need the extra benefits. Don't pay for services you won't use, no matter how neatly packaged the offer.

- Use your credit cards only for necessary purchases. Don't charge toys, liquor, or vacations. If you can't pay cash, you don't need them at the moment.

- If you're making a major purchase on a credit card, select a card that charges a lower interest rate.

- Review your credit card statements carefully each month. Attend to mistakes or questions about your bill promptly.

- Pay the entire bill on every credit card every month.
- Reduce the amount of credit available to you. Cancel credit cards you don't need.
- Consolidate your credit card debt so that you pay interest charges on only one card.
- Pay off outstanding credit card balances before taking on further debt. Re-evaluate the amount of debt you're willing to carry in relation to the amount of money you want to save.
- Pay off the credit cards with the highest interest rates first.

Debt

The later section "How to Assess Your Situation" provides guidelines to help you determine whether your debt is enough to worry about. However, any debt is too much if you're not completely comfortable with it. If you can't easily pay all your bills every month, or if you carry a balance on any of your credit cards, you're already wading into the bog. If you don't do something to change your direction, you'll be in over your head before you know it.

Debts are broken down into a variety of categories. Understanding and identifying these categories can help you prioritize your payments and identify places to cut back. All debts are either secured or unsecured.

Secured loans

A *secured loan* is a loan backed by collateral — something of value that you own and pledge to a lender to insure payment. You make a promise, usually in the form of a printed security agreement, stating that the creditor, or person or company you owe money to, can take a specified item of your property if you fail to pay back the loan.

Often, the item pledged is the one being purchased. The pledged item can also be an item you already own. If you stop paying for any reason, the pledged item goes to the creditor.

The most common items purchased by a secured loan are

- Houses, condos, land, and cottages
- Motor vehicles (cars, trucks, vans, and motorcycles)
- Major appliances and electronics (refrigerators, washing machines, televisions, and computers)
- Furniture and power tools
- Valuable jewellery

Generally speaking, secured loans are high priorities in your debt repayment plan, especially if the loans are for a home or transportation. You may be willing to have someone repossess a diamond necklace, but you don't want anyone foreclosing on your mortgage and repossessing your home.

Unsecured loans

An *unsecured loan* is a loan not backed by collateral — anything you own that can be taken by the lender if you can't pay the debt. The majority of debt in Canada is in the form of unsecured loans — primarily credit cards — but this category also includes student and personal loans, and dental bills. (Personal loans are unsecured loans you take out to pay for specific expenditures, such as a vacation or a wedding.) The lender grants you credit based on your creditworthiness or, in some cases, on the creditworthiness of a co-signer (someone who agrees to repay the loan if you are unable to).

Because unsecured loans are riskier for lenders, most of these loans have higher interest rates than secured loans do. Due to high interest rates, particularly on credit cards, these loans can represent the biggest drain on your finances.

Expenses

Expense is spending or cost — just another form of debt, really. But expense is traditionally short term, like food costs or the phone bill. (Of course, putting expenses on a credit card makes them part of your "real" debts, with the increased possibility of added interest payments.)

Many sources use the terms *expense* and *debt* interchangeably, so understand that whichever term is used it always ends up meaning money is going out.

Essential expenses

Some expenses must be paid, either because of the law or because you still need someplace to live — even if you're broke. These essential expenses fall into two categories: essential fixed expenses and essential variable expenses.

Essential fixed expenses don't vary from month to month. You may see annual increases in some categories, but you can often anticipate these expenses and plan for them. Essential fixed expenses include the following:

- Rent or mortgage payments
- Car payments
- Insurance (auto, health, life)
- Alimony/child support
- Taxes

Essential variable expenses differ from month to month, but they often offer you a greater opportunity to cut costs, either by finding less expensive alternatives or by cutting back on use. Essential variable expenses include the following:

- Food
- Utilities (water, gas, electricity)
- Phone

- Gasoline or other transportation costs
- Health care expenses
- More taxes!

Other payments, such as debt repayment, are not normally included under essential expenses because these payments are not considered part of an "ideal" budget. They include payments on secured loans (other than home equity or improvement loans and mortgage), unsecured loans, student loans, personal loans, and instalment payment plans.

Because your goal is to be debt-free and have a beautifully unblemished credit report, you want to keep repaying your debts.

Now's the time for a few words about an essential expense: taxes. Most of the time, adequate taxes are deducted from your paycheque. But if you find at the end of the year that you owe taxes, the expense can add to your debt burden. If you're self-employed, the expense may become a problem even before the end of the tax year. Either way, you need to keep a few things in mind when you're trying to prioritize your payments:

- Paying taxes is always and unequivocally essential, if for no other reason than it's the law. More than almost anyone else, the Canada Revenue Agency (CRA) can make your life complicated.

- That said, know the CRA wants to help you pay your taxes. The CRA offers a number of useful taxpayer information publications, and can refer you to free tax services. Also, the CRA can help you put together a payment schedule for paying your taxes.

Nonessential expenses

Just about everything that's not listed in the earlier section "Essential expenses" is nonessential. Some services, conveniences, and luxuries have become such a normal part of everyday life you may think they're essential, but they're not.

Popular nonessentials include

- Cable TV
- Lawn services
- Cleaning services
- Magazine subscriptions (unless they're business related)
- Cigarettes, alcohol, and lattes
- Restaurant meals
- Movies (especially full-priced ones) and sporting events
- Non-basic cell phone plans
- Expensive hairstyling
- Designer clothes
- Club memberships

Borderline/debatable expenses

Just as one person's meat is another person's poison, so, too, one person's nonessential expense can be another person's necessity. Because no one else possesses precisely the same combination of characteristics, needs, priorities, and circumstances that you do, some expenses — perhaps many — require careful consideration. Be honest with yourself about what you really need, and what you simply are accustomed to or find convenient.

An expense is considered borderline or debatable when, due to circumstances or life situation, it cannot easily be dropped into either the essential or the nonessential category. Borderline expenses may be nonessential in themselves, but you may be nearly finished paying for something with no hope of regaining your investment. They may be debts owed to people you can talk into waiting a little while longer for repayment. Also, some essential expenses (such as a phone) have extra features (such as three-way calling) that are nonessential in most cases.

Following are examples of expenses that may be borderline or debatable:

- If you're young and healthy, permanent life insurance is debatable. Consider term life insurance until you're out of debt.

- Health club membership may be debatable. If you just signed up and owe thousands, dump the membership. If you paid a huge, nonrefundable initiation fee several years ago and pay only a small monthly or annual maintenance fee now, the membership is probably worth keeping — especially if you use the health club as a low-cost alternative to costlier activities.

- Health and auto insurance may be essential, but low deductibles aren't. Find out whether you can lower your payments by having a higher deductible. Make sure to budget for extra savings to cover the higher deductible.

- Clothes are less debatable than you may think. For most people (other than growing children), clothes don't need to be replaced that often. Consider sticking with what you have for a couple of years unless something disintegrates or you have to go on a job interview and you don't have anything appropriate to wear.

Identifying your expense types

To identify how your expenses and debts can be categorized, write down everything on which you spend money. Include as much detail as possible in your list, making the list as long as necessary.

Although big purchases obviously cause greater debt, the little, unplanned things — the ones you hardly even notice — are often the ones that undercut your best intentions. For example, snacking out of vending machines combined with stopping for gourmet coffee on the way to work each day can add up to nearly $2,000 a year — and that's after-tax money, so you have to earn $3,000 before you have $6 to blow each day on a luxury treat.

Using the following codes, identify the status of each expense item on your list:

- S = Secured loan
- U = Unsecured loan
- EF = Essential fixed expense
- EV = Essential variable expense
- N = Nonessential expense
- R = Expense that can be reduced
- C = Expense that can be cut entirely
- ? = Need to research whether this expense can be reduced or cut

Note: You don't see a code for borderline/debatable items because items are borderline only until you decide which category they belong in. Making that decision is one of the things you need to accomplish in this exercise.

Table 1-3 gives you an idea of how your worksheet may look.

Item	Category
Mortgage	S, EF, ?
Food	EV, R
Phone, general	EV, R
Phone, extras	
Entertainment	
Magazines	
Gasoline	
Health club	
Beverages purchased at/to/from office	
Car payment	
Life insurance	
Personal loan(s)	
Cable TV	

Table 1-3: *Items on Which You Spend Money*

Continue to add lines, making the list as long as necessary. You want to account for everything on which you spend money.

This chart is not a contract. Expenses do not need to remain static. As circumstances change, you can add or delete items or change the status of an item. If a job change makes it necessary for you to have a tablet, for example, you can simply move that expense from the nonessential to the essential category.

For the next few days, you may want to keep notes and jot down items you didn't think to add to your expense list. (Those items could include the laundry money you always toss in a jar so you'll have it when you need it or the drink you have with friends every Friday night.) The more aware you are of where your money goes, the easier it will be to keep your expenses under control.

By the time you're through with this worksheet, you'll have a good idea of where your money is going, what you must include in your budget, and where you can cut back. You can reduce most expenses if you put your mind to it. The more you do so, the more quickly you can improve your credit history.

How to Assess Your Situation

One thing is true for everyone: To plan how to get somewhere, you have to know where you're starting. That's why you need to start by assessing your financial situation.

How you got into debt is particularly significant because the work you need to do and the changes you want to make will be different if, for example, your debts were caused by job loss as opposed to uncontrolled spending. Determining your priorities will help you later in the budgeting and rebuilding process (see Chapter 2).

Figure out how much you owe

You can set your repayment priorities later. Right now, you need to figure out where you stand in the negative column.

Total debt

Use Table 1-4 to record all your debts. Total your debts by type, and then calculate your grand total. This final number represents your total outstanding debt. If an item in the sample worksheet doesn't apply to you, skip it; also feel free to add or delete items so the worksheet accurately reflects your debt. Also, add the percentage interest rate being charged for each credit card and loan next to the amount due.

Home Debt	Amount Due	Annual Interest Rate %
Mortgage		
Home equity loan		
Furniture on instalment plan		
Appliances on instalment plan		
Past-due utility bills		
Total home debt		
Auto Debt	**Amount Due**	**Annual Interest Rate %**
Loan/car 1		
Loan/car 2		
Total auto debt		
Credit Card Debt	**Amount Due**	**Annual Interest Rate %**
Mastercard		
Visa		
Other		
(Add as many other lines as necessary)		
Total credit card debt		

Table 1-4: *Calculating Your Total Debt*

(continued)

Miscellaneous Debt	Amount Due	Annual Interest Rate %
Personal loans		
Student loans		
Other loans		
Total miscellaneous debt		
Outstanding Taxes	**Amount Due**	**Annual Interest Rate %**
Federal		
Provincial		
Municipal		
Other		
Total tax debt		
Total all debts		

Table 1-4: *(continued)*

Notice you don't have to include regular expenses such as utilities (unless they're past due), food, and fuel. That's because, even though these expenses arise regularly, they really aren't part of your debt (unless you charge them). However, they do have an impact on how much money is available to go toward your debts. So don't get rid of any information you have on these expenses, because you'll need it when you do your budget. (See Chapter 2.)

Rent and lease payments are also excluded, because they are not debt in the same sense a loan is — though you are legally obligated to pay both even if you give up the apartment or car. Also, alimony and child support are not included. Although these are all debt obligations if you owe them, and have to be part of your calculations, they are not things you can pay off early or reduce.

Debt as percentage of income

To determine how serious your debt is, you need to determine how much of your monthly net income (that's income after taxes — your actual take-home pay) is going toward paying debt. To do so, follow these steps:

1. **Add up your monthly debt obligations, including rent or mortgage payment, lease or car loan payments, other loan payments, credit card payments, alimony, and child support.**

2. **Divide the total by the amount of your monthly income after taxes.**

3. **Unlike the total debt amount you calculated earlier, for this calculation consider only the monthly payments you make.**

For example, imagine you have a mortgage payment of $800, an automobile loan payment of $300, a credit card payment of $100, a student loan payment of $200, an instalment loan payment of $100, and take-home pay of $4,500. Here's how this monthly debt obligation translates into debt as percentage of income:

- $800 + $300 + $100 + $200 + $100 = $1,500 in monthly debt obligations
- $1,500 ÷ $4,500 = 33.3 percent

In other words, 33.3 percent of the monthly net income ($4,500) goes toward paying off debt.

If your debt obligations are 25 percent or less of your take-home pay, you're in reasonable shape. If they're between 25 and 35 percent, you should be concerned and begin thinking about how you can try to get closer to 25 percent or less. If they're over 35 percent, you're headed for serious trouble or may already be there — you must move quickly and decisively to reduce debt. The 33.3 percent in the sample formula, therefore, is not yet catastrophic but is well into the "time to get serious about debt" range.

On a card or piece of notepaper, write your current percentage, then write next to it the percentage to aim for (25 percent or less). Write today's date on the card, and write down how long you think it will take you to achieve your goals. (Don't worry, you can always revise this estimate as you progress.) Place it somewhere you can see it regularly, to help you keep your goal in mind.

Write down how you got into debt

It's possible you played no part in the accumulation of debt — you may have inherited it from others or acquired it as a result of circumstances beyond your control, such as a serious illness, an accident, or a natural disaster. In that case, you simply need to address the mechanics of paying bills and rebuilding credit. With the disciplines of a few money-saving and debt-retiring strategies, you may find yourself in a stronger position than before your debts accrued.

Most people, however, have a pattern of debt — a series of behaviours that get them into the hole. The more uncertain you are of how you got into trouble, the more likely it is you'll need to change some of your behaviours. If you're not as debt-averse as you should be, recognizing this as a risk factor is the first step to getting yourself fiscally fit.

This important exercise will help you determine how you got into debt. You need to be really honest with yourself for this to work. If you've run up thousands of dollars in credit card debt, don't call it "bad luck." Get a sheet of paper and start to write down behaviours or triggers that get you into trouble. Don't judge yourself or your debts as you write. No one else needs to see this list. Simply write down everything that's fuelling your debt.

To get started on your list, answer the following questions:

- Why did you take on your first significant debt load?
- How do you feel about debt?
- How does spending money make you feel?
- Do you ever "binge shop"? If so, what sorts of things trigger the binges?

- What reaction do you have to advertisements for items you want but can't afford?
- Do you believe that paying the minimum amount on your credit card will get the balance paid off?
- Are you ever surprised by how high a bill is?
- Do you forget about money you've spent?
- Do you balance your chequing account regularly?
- Do you have any expensive hobbies or habits?
- Do you feel competitive with or threatened by those around you?
- How often do you eat out?
- When you eat out with friends, do you collect cash from others, charge the meal, and then buy something else with the cash instead of paying down your credit card debt?
- Do you plan your purchases, or do you buy on impulse?

Review your list on how much you owe. The information may give you even more ideas about how you got into debt. Add any discoveries to your list of trouble behaviours and triggers.

As you write, more ideas may come to you. Record everything that crosses your mind regarding your spending habits, whether it's a feeling that you must pamper yourself to deal with stress, a hope that you can overcome your sense of dissatisfaction with life, or a belief that you need to impress someone.

 A journal can be particularly helpful in identifying emotion-triggered spending, as well as in tracking your progress and recording what you learn, both about the process and about yourself.

As you continue through the rest of this book, add to your list any new information you discover about yourself. Knowing why you spend and what your triggers are can help you figure out how to stop uncontrolled spending.

Determine your priorities

Obviously, one major priority is to get out of debt. At this point, however, you need to think about what your priorities in life are; how they relate to or may be affected by debt; and how they fit into the process of getting out of debt.

For this exercise, think about your real priorities — the things that matter deeply to you. You need to account for considerations like family and beliefs first and foremost, no matter what type of debt you're facing.

Later, when you start to create your budget (see Chapter 2), you can prioritize your "wish list" — the things you would like but that aren't really vital in the greater scheme of things — in order to identify expenses you can reduce or cut. But right now, think about the priorities that will help you determine what kind of path you will take.

Here are some questions to answer as you think about your priorities:

- Where does your family fit into the picture?

- Is taking a second job an option (financially, emotionally)?

- Is giving to charity or religious organizations important to you?

- For your own peace of mind, how quickly do you want to be out of debt? What are you willing to sacrifice to get there?

- What things that are important to you are affected by your debt, or may be affected by it if you do not remedy it? (This may include anything from not being able to join friends for dinner to having to postpone starting a family or losing your house.)

- What goals do you have that may be attainable when you're out of debt? (This could be anything from educating children to enjoying a comfortable retirement.)

As you think about your priorities, jot down the things that matter most to you — the things that will have an impact on how and why you want to get out of debt.

For example, if you have young children or aging parents, you may not view a second job as an option. In this case, you're making family a priority and accepting the possibility of a slightly longer repayment period. The debts aren't going anywhere but the people are, so this is a good choice. Getting in or out of debt is about making your life better, not worse.

Look at your resources and assets

In evaluating the resources and assets you have for getting yourself out of debt, consider not only your income but also any capital available, including savings, investments, and property. This exercise has two steps:

1. **Calculate your monthly income.**

   You'll use this figure later to work out your budget. Because income can change over time, the wisest approach is simply to figure out what you're taking in at the present time.

2. **Determine any additional funds that may be available to you.**

   If you need to make dramatic changes in your debt profile, also consider potential sources of money.

Set up your calculations something like Table 1-5, with the various real or potential sources of funds separated.

Reviewing your assets helps you determine where your money is, which in turn helps you with both the budgeting process and improving your debt picture (see Chapter 2).

Income (After Taxes)	Amount
Primary wages	
Secondary wages (second job/secondary wage earner)	
Alimony/child support	
Government support	
Other income	
Total income	
Easily Accessible Money	**Amount**
Savings	
Investments	
Total easily accessible money	
Less Accessible Money	**Amount**
Home equity	
Car equity	
Boat equity	
Other (such as equity in a vacation home or undeveloped property)	
Cash-value insurance	
Total less accessible money	
Other Possible (Though Less Desirable) Sources of Money	**Amount**
RRSPs	
Total other sources of money	

Table 1-5: *Calculating Your Total Assets*

2

Getting Out of Debt

Your first steps to managing your money are to figure out your goals and to assess the debt that might prevent you from achieving those goals. In Chapter 1, you determine where you are in terms of your goals and your debt — your starting point. Your goals are about where you're going. Now it's time to plan the trip. This process includes setting specific debt management goals, determining how long the journey should take, and creating a map to help you get there.

How to Put Together a Budget

Your budget helps you do two things: plan your spending and track your progress. A budget may seem restrictive at first, but it frees you from the worry of not knowing how you're doing financially. A budget can give you greater control and keep you on the road to your destination — freedom from debt. Budgets are great vehicles to help you get where you want to be, but they require a special fuel — your commitment.

Determine and refine your debt repayment goals

Setting goals takes effort and commitment. You need to think carefully about where you want to be financially, as well as what future plans you have that may be affected by your finances. You also need to be reasonable, and not set yourself impossible goals. Take this seriously, but don't panic about it — you can modify your goals as time goes by. Setting goals is not meant to be a nasty straitjacket.

The following sections discuss the key elements you will need to consider to create goals that are both attainable and motivating.

Be positive

Your goal shouldn't be something negative, such as "to spend less money." Staying motivated by a negative goal is difficult. Charting your progress is also difficult — when have you cut enough? To be effective, your goal needs to be an accomplishment, not a sacrifice.

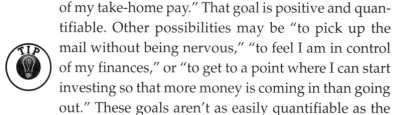

Instead, your goal should be something like "to enjoy the freedom of carrying a debt load of only 25 percent of my take-home pay." That goal is positive and quantifiable. Other possibilities may be "to pick up the mail without being nervous," "to feel I am in control of my finances," or "to get to a point where I can start investing so that more money is coming in than going out." These goals aren't as easily quantifiable as the percentage-of-take-home-pay goal, but the point is to find something that keeps you motivated and excited about the process.

Take your plans into account

In a way, you've already established one goal: to be out of debt. Although this is your primary goal, you may want to consider other, secondary goals, which will be made possible by your success with your primary goal.

Depending on where you are in life, your plans may be to have children, buy a house, put children through university, or enjoy a secure retirement. All these goals will benefit — and some are only possible — if you get your finances under control. The nearer in time your plans lie, the more quickly you want to eliminate your debt and begin saving. For example, if you want to buy a house in five years, you may be willing to work harder to pay off your credit cards so you can get a mortgage. And you may even want to give yourself an extra year or two to save up for furniture so you don't get into too much debt again.

 Over time, your lifestyle, earning power, and attitudes may change, so review your goals regularly to make sure they still reflect your plans.

Establish a time frame

The general structure of goal-setting is to establish immediate goals, intermediate goals, and long-term goals:

- **Immediate goals** are goals that you expect to accomplish in the next few weeks, such as finishing your budget, getting started on paying debts, and making necessary adjustments to your spending.

- **Intermediate goals** are goals that need to be set at regular intervals — every six months, for example. At these intervals, you can review your accomplishments and reassess your direction. But, as always, these should also be specific goals, such as "Pay off credit card X by this date."

- **Long-term goals** are the goals that take you to the end of your debt problems and beyond. These goals may include getting to a point where you have no credit card debt, followed by having your debt in the 25 percent range, possibly followed by paying off your mortgage or building future wealth or both.

You can always adjust the dates if you don't accomplish everything you planned by a given date — or if you're paying off debts faster than you expected. These time goals aren't carved in stone but rather are goalposts — you try to get the ball between the posts, but it doesn't always happen. Without goalposts, however, you'll never know whether you scored.

Make sure to allow yourself a realistic amount of time to get out of debt. You probably didn't get into debt overnight, and you certainly won't get out of debt overnight. Different factors can contribute to getting out of debt in more time or less, including your level of net income, your take-home pay, and your level of commitment to the process.

Write down your goals

Plenty of good reasons exist for writing down anything that's important:

- You tend to remember information better if you take the time to write it down.

- You're more likely to believe something you see written out. Seeing it on paper makes it real, concrete, and tangible.

- You have something to look at, which makes it harder to forget or ignore that you've made a decision.

- You have proof that you've already accomplished an important task. Goal-setting is a major step in the process of getting out of debt, and when you've set the goal, you can start getting excited about the destination.

Write your positive, long-term goal statement at the top of a sheet of paper. Below it, write the dates you've set for attaining your short-term, intermediate, and long-term goals.

If you haven't already started a file or three-ring binder for the project of getting out of debt, now is a good time to do so. Place your sheet of written goals in the front of the binder or file. This way, you have everything you need in one place: goals, worksheets, and any other information you collect.

In addition to the sheet of paper listing your goals that you put in your file or binder, you can write your positive, long-term goal statement on a 3-x-5-inch card and post it where you'll see it regularly, such as on the bathroom mirror.

For this reminder note, you can rephrase the statement in a less formal way. For example, instead of "In five years, I want to have my debt to 25 percent of my take-home pay," you may write it as "In five years, if I stick with this, I can be free!" Write whatever gets you the most excited about this process. You can then rewrite the note every time you reach an intermediate goal ("Just four more years!"). Updating your note helps keep you out of the "Are we there yet?" syndrome that accompanies many long-term projects.

Create a budget

By creating your budget, you draw your road map for getting out of debt. No single perfect form fits everyone's needs and circumstances, but you do need to consider some basic elements if your budget is going to work. An effective budget needs to be realistic, concise, flexible, and open:

- **Realistic:** Forcing numbers to work out on paper isn't hard, but these numbers need to work in real life.

Even if you need to watch every penny at this point, don't make the numbers so low that you have no hope of succeeding. If, as you go along, you find ways of cutting costs further, you can always change an entry.

- **Concise yet comprehensive:** You don't want your budget to have so much detail that you spend your entire life keeping it updated, but you do want to include all expenses you can identify or predict.

You often can group several expenses into one category. Although you may need to track expenses more precisely from day to day (you may even want to carry a notebook in which to record them or use the notes app on your smartphone), you can consolidate some items in the budget. For example, coffee from the gourmet shop, candy from the office vending machine, and a litre of milk picked up on the way home can all be part of the food budget. See Chapter 3 for more tips about figuring out what you spend.

- **Flexible:** Feel free to improve the format of the budget as you continue to work with it. Add more lines if necessary, or delete lines. Change your spending estimates as needed, too. You may find you guessed too low, or you may discover ways to save money that enable you to lower an amount.

If your financial situation changes — you get married, find a new job, relocate, or have a new mouth to feed — you may want to draw up a new budget.

- **Open to all concerned, garnering everyone's cooperation and commitment:** Anyone in the household who contributes to income or expenditures or both needs to be involved in the budget discussions. In particular, those who contribute to the household income need to get in on the planning stages, budget creation, and review process. They need to buy in to the project for it to work.

Small children may not need to be included in the planning, but they should know that something is happening because the budget will affect them, too. If they feel as though they're part of the project, they may be more understanding when you can't buy things for them. In fact, small children can get excited about being involved and may want to contribute by saving their allowance, collecting pop bottles, or finding other ways to contribute to the family's success.

To establish your budget, you first want to create a master copy of the budget worksheet (see upcoming Table 2-1) with no numbers filled in. You may want to include a few blank lines in each category on the master, in case you need to add other items later. Then photocopy this master document to create budget worksheets to work on.

A dozen copies (one for each month) is a good start, because you'll want to work within a budget for at least a year. Even if you can get yourself to that magic 25 percent figure in less time, living on a budget for a year helps create a budget mindset that keeps you from falling back into the hole you just climbed out of. Some people live on a budget their entire lives because it's the only way they keep themselves out of trouble. You may not have to do so, but if it helps, it's an option.

Your worksheet also needs to be well organized and easy to read and keep updated. If working with the budget and calculating totals become difficult, you'll almost certainly give up. This process is serious, so make the effort to create a document that's easy to work with.

Although you'll personalize this worksheet to meet your own needs, some categories need to be a part of everyone's budget. Also, some organizational options may make the budget easier for you to manage. Be sure to do the following:

- Include a space after each item for estimated expense, actual expense, and the difference between estimated and actual.

- Divide the budget worksheet into essential and non-essential expenses (see Chapter 1). You may want to further divide essential expenses into fixed and variable; doing so makes it easier to see where you may need to make changes to the budget or to your spending. (Chapter 1 helps you create a list of debts and expenses that can help you accomplish this task. Just check the category you indicated for each item.)

- After the total for the expense section, list your sources of income and total them.

- The final entry on the budget is the calculation of money remaining. Subtract your total expenses from your total income to determine what remains. The remainder is called your discretionary income.

Table 2-1 gives you an idea of what your budget might look like. Feel free to alter the format to meet your own needs, but be sure to include enough information to make the budget effective. And don't forget any debatable items that may not be listed in the table. Also, if you have regular legal or accounting expenses, don't forget to include them.

Note that on the sample budget, no blank lines appear under the loan and credit card categories. The simple reason is that you should not be adding items to these categories. If all goes as planned, you'll be eliminating debt categories, not adding them.

You can use the blank lines under the Other expense and income categories for seasonal expenses or annual bills, such as auto licences, vacations, holiday gift purchases, bonuses, and tax preparation services.

Expense	Estimated	Actual	Difference
Essential Fixed Expenses			
Rent/mortgage			
Housing association fees			
Car payment			
Car insurance			
Life insurance			
Homeowner's/renter's insurance			
Property taxes			
Alimony/child support			
Other			
Other			
Essential Variable Expenses			
Home maintenance			
Food			
Electricity			
Gas (utility)			
Water			
Phone			
Gasoline (auto)			
Auto maintenance/repairs			
Public transportation			
Health care expenses			
Child care			
Charitable donations			
Household goods (cleaning supplies, cooking utensils, and so on)			
Savings			

Table 2-1: *Budget Worksheet for (Month)*

Expense	Estimated	Actual	Difference
Other			
Other			
Fixed Loan Payments			
Student loan			
Personal loan			
Instalment loan 1			
Credit Card Payments			
Mastercard 1			
Mastercard 2			
Visa 1			
Visa 2			
Department store cards			
Gasoline cards			
Other cards			
Charge cards (cards that must be paid off each month)			
American Express (regular)			
Diners Club			
Nonessential Expenses			
Barber/beautician			
Magazine/newspaper subscriptions			
Gifts			
Charitable donations			
Cable TV			
Club dues			

(continued)

Expense	Estimated	Actual	Difference
Sports			
Lessons/camp			
Dining out			
Movies			
Hobbies			
Cigarettes			
Alcoholic beverages			
Domestic help			
Lawn services			
Other			
Other			
Total Monthly Expenses			
Monthly Income			
Take-home pay (after taxes)			
Interest income			
Alimony/child support paid to you			
Other			
Other			
Other			
Total Monthly Income			
Total Money Remaining			
Total Monthly Income			
Total Monthly Expenses			
Total Money Remaining			

Table 2-1: *(continued)*

If you're self-employed, don't forget to list estimated quarterly taxes under Essential Fixed Expenses.

After you create your own budget worksheet and make copies of the blank form, plug in figures. You'll know some numbers immediately, especially the fixed expenses. (Chapter 1 has worksheets you can use to record your income and assets and where you spend your money, which will help you prepare your budget.) Be as accurate and realistic as possible when filling in amounts.

 For utility prices, you can phone your local utility companies. They often can tell you precisely what your average monthly costs have been. Utility companies may also offer a payment plan where you pay the average of your annual bills every month rather than dealing with seasonal dips and rises. Averaged payments can make the budgeting process much easier.

All these figures go in the Estimated column, because it's what you're predicting your costs will be or what you think you'll be able to put toward paying off your debts. (*Note:* For fixed essential expenses, for most of the year the Estimated column will match the Actual column, but they are still included because it will be easier when you total the columns.) Work in pencil so you can erase entries if necessary. Put down the minimum payment amounts for all credit cards, unless you regularly set and pay a higher amount.

Finally, with all the items in the Estimated column filled in, total your expenses and income and then figure your remaining money.

Evaluate your budget

If your Total Money Remaining figure is zero or negative, you definitely have to revise your budget. First, examine your non-essential expenses. Which ones can be reduced? Which ones can be eliminated? Keep working until you can't think of anything else to reduce. Be honest with yourself about what you can and can't give up or reduce. You don't need a $65 haircut or cable TV, for example. To succeed, however, focus not on what you're giving up but on what you're gaining: eventual economic freedom.

If you do have money remaining, you can use it to help get yourself out of debt faster, as explained in the later section "How to Use Your Budget to Get Ahead of Your Debt." If cutting or reducing nonessentials isn't enough to get you into a positive situation, you may need to start examining your essential expenses. Check out the later section "Improve Your Debt Picture by Moving Money" to discover how to find more money in your budget.

Stay up-to-date

Setting up your budget is just the beginning of your move to financial freedom. Keeping your budget going takes less work than setting it up, but it requires more commitment.

As the month progresses and bills come in, fill in the Actual column for each item and calculate the difference between the estimated amount and the actual amount, noting whether the difference is positive or negative.

Set aside time every month to total the preceding month's worksheet and to review (and update if necessary) your budget for the coming month. You can make seasonal adjustments to anticipate times when spending may be higher, or fine-tune entries as you get better at living according to a budget.

Stay up-to-date by making a commitment to the following:

- **Regularity:** Only by being systematic and by updating your records regularly can you get a good picture of your spending patterns. Being consistent helps you know where your money is going and how you're progressing. Also, if you fall behind, catching up may appear to be a discouragingly difficult task.

- **Accuracy:** You don't have to worry about every penny, but try to be as accurate as possible in recording amounts. Carrying a paper notebook or using a notes app on your smartphone can help you because otherwise you may not remember every trip to the pop

machine, coffee cart, or vending machine — the types
of expenses that can add several dollars to each day's
expense total.

- **Honesty:** If you're anything less than honest when figuring your budget, you're hurting only yourself. If you
record less than what you spend, you will never have
accurate records and you may never succeed in getting
out of debt. Knowing your true financial picture is the
only way to make a budget work.

How to Use Your Budget to Get Ahead of Your Debt

When you have a budget in hand, along with a picture of your
debt situation, you can strategize about how best to tackle your
debt. This section tells you how to get started, giving you strategies for reducing your debt and preventing yourself from getting even further into debt.

Pay off high-interest debts first with your discretionary income

Discretionary income is the money you have left after you've
paid all the bills you have to pay — the Total Money Remaining
figure at the end of your budget worksheet (refer to Table 2-1).

This money is the income that you use at your discretion for extras, from treats to investing, unless you're in debt.

The budget you created includes items that may normally fall into the discretionary income category (movies, dining out, and so on) simply because at this stage you have to plan all your expenses. Depending on your level of debt, you may not have much discretionary income after you account for all the items on your budget. If you do have some money to spare, you can use it to help get out of debt faster. This process cuts down on one of the worst drains of money — compounding interest payments.

The single most devastating expense you have is the interest on credit cards. Most people don't realize how much they pay in interest or how much difference even the smallest changes can make.

Here's an example: Say you have a credit card that has a balance of $1,500. If the annual interest is 21 percent (a fairly standard rate) and you make the minimum payment of 3 percent of the balance each month, repaying the total will take you more than 14 years, and you will have paid more than $1,800 in interest (for a total of $3,300).

If you pay just $5 over the minimum payment per month, you'll save more than $600 on interest and cut more than five years off the repayment time. If you pay $10 more per month, you'll cut nearly $900 and eight years off the interest and time that making only the minimum payment hits you with.

Those numbers show a dramatic difference. And these figures are based on the assumption that you don't spend any more after you run up the initial $1,500. If you keep adding purchases, they all figure into the interest rate.

To keep your creditors at bay, you must continue to make the minimum payment due on each card on which you owe. After you account for those expenses, any discretionary income you have left in your budget (the amount in the Total Money Remaining column back in Table 2-1) should go toward paying off the credit cards that have the highest interest rates.

If you planned your budget with more than the minimum payment going to each card with an outstanding balance, redo it so that you're paying the minimum on the cards with lower interest rates and putting the rest of your extra money toward paying off the highest cards. Follow these steps:

1. **After you create your budget and plug in the minimum payment for each credit card, take as much of your discretionary income as possible and use it to pay down the credit card charging the highest interest.**

 If you wrote the interest rates on your debt worksheet in Chapter 1, you'll be able to tell at a glance which credit card you need to target.

2. **After you've paid off the credit card with the highest rate, put your discretionary income toward the credit card with the next highest rate.**

3. **Continue this process until you've paid off all your credit cards, continuing to put as much discretionary income as possible toward the card with the highest interest rate.**

Discretionary income, as its name implies, is money you can use at your discretion. Occasionally, you may want to reserve a little more discretionary income to celebrate the holidays or enjoy a much-needed weekend away. However, until you're getting cozy with that 25 percent debt figure, you want to plow as much of your discretionary income as possible into paying off high-interest debts.

Think of paying off high-interest debts as saving your future buying power, because that's precisely what it is. Nothing eats into your financial potential like a high interest rate. Also remember that paying off debts is a good thing to do to improve your credit rating. Your rating goes up as your debt goes down — and vice versa. As soon as you show you don't need debt, you can easily get some new debt — if that's a fiscal direction you want to follow.

What you've been reading about so far is consumer debt, which is bad. What you want to have is investment debt, which is good. Yes, it's true: All debts are not created equal.

Cut up your credit cards

Here comes the hard part: As soon as you've paid off the balance on a credit card, cut up the card and close the account with a quick phone call to the credit card company.

You may not be able to take the scissors to every credit card you have (because it's nearly impossible to transact business these days without at least one major credit card), but do so with the majority of your cards. Plan to keep one or two of the major cards (Visa, Mastercard, or American Express) and get rid of everything else.

In fact, you probably should cut up all but the chosen two cards as soon as you start working on eliminating your debt. (Cutting up a card doesn't mean you erase the balance, of course, but it does prevent you from making additional purchases on the card.) Whatever you do, don't charge anything while you're still carrying a balance; it just makes the interest worse and the repayment time longer.

Consider getting a new card with no balance. Use this card only when you can't use cash or a cheque, and charge only an amount that you can pay off completely when the bill arrives. Because your goal is never again to carry a balance on a credit card, you absolutely do not want to start running up another balance.

Forget your savings for the time being

While you're seriously in debt is the only time in your life that anyone will tell you your nest egg is a bad idea. If you have any money in a savings account, close the account and put the money toward paying off your high-interest credit cards.

Why earn 1 or 2 percent interest on a savings account, and pay tax on the interest, too, when you're paying 17 to 21 percent interest on your credit cards and getting no tax deduction?

Liquidate any other assets you have, such as guaranteed investment certificates (GICs), shares, bonds, mutual funds, and even collectibles, and use that money to pay down your high-interest debts as well. Nothing can earn you enough to make it worth staying in debt on a credit card that charges a 19 percent interest rate. Don't forget: For you to have 19 percent after tax, you have to earn about 30 percent before tax. That is huge.

Only two exceptions to the "throw everything at your credit cards" plan exist:

- Hang on to enough money to cover one month's expenses (if possible), because emergencies do arise. If you can't scrape together a month's worth, at least save enough to buy food and gas and to pay for shelter (mortgage, rent).

- As long as you can still make the minimum payments on all your debts, don't cash in your registered retirement savings plans (RRSPs). The tax hit would probably be worse than the interest on your credit cards. Also, jeopardizing your future simply to avoid interest payments is not a wise trade-off.

  If you're facing foreclosure, however, that's another matter. Go ahead and liquidate all your assets, including retirement accounts; you don't want to lose your home.

Pay down other debts

If you stick to your budget, you'll free yourself of credit card debt. At that point, you may still have other debts to deal with, such as auto loans, student loans, and a mortgage loan. Even if you're close to that 25 percent debt figure, you may still want to rid yourself of debt entirely.

To do so, simply follow the same procedure for high-interest debt just described: Continue to choose the debt with the highest interest and put as much of your discretionary income as possible toward that debt. As you pay off debts, be sure to update your budget and reallocate your resources. Also make sure not to neglect other debts while you focus on the highest-interest one; you don't want to lose your car or your home by failing to make your monthly payments.

Some types of loans, such as mortgages, assess a pre-payment penalty if you pay off the loan early. Make sure to read the fine print on your loan agreement before you end up costing yourself more than you're saving!

Improve Your Debt Picture by Moving Money

One thing you can do to get a slightly faster start along the path to reaching your final goal of being debt-free is to move your money to where it can do the most good. This tactic includes everything from finding ways to lower your interest payments to locating and plugging the leaks in your budget that let money get away from you. This section shows you how to do all that and more.

Find cheaper debt

In addition to paying off your high-interest debts, you may also be able to find lower-interest debts to help you get out of debt faster. The following are some sources of cheaper debt.

Lower-interest credit cards

How often do you get offers for credit cards with really low interest rates? Probably almost daily. If you've never taken advantage of these low rates (or you took advantage of them and just ran up more debt), it may be time for you to look at these offers again.

Of course, these reduced rates are usually for a limited time only, so check the offer to make sure the post–hot deal interest rate isn't higher than what you're paying now. But if the rate is the same or lower than what you're currently paying, you'll come out ahead even if you can't pay off the entire debt during the trial period.

In addition, some credit cards have a regular interest rate that's lower than the rate on the majority of cards. If you don't have a brochure for a great deal on a new credit card, you can research some of the better rates available by going online.

After you transfer balances from the higher-interest to the lower-interest cards, cut up the old cards, and close the accounts. The only potential exception is an emergency backup card with a zero balance. Otherwise, do "plastic surgery" and get rid of as many cards as possible.

 Don't just throw your cards out. You need to confirm by telephone or by mail that the account has been closed and removed from your credit report.

Credit union loans

If you belong to a credit union, find out what types of loans are available. You may be able to get a personal loan at a rate far lower than what you're paying in credit card interest. If you've been a member in good standing for some time, you can often get a loan at a rate lower than what a bank would offer.

Mortgage refinancing

Refinancing a mortgage is advantageous because it can not only free up money for your current difficulties but also lower your payments for the duration of the mortgage. This strategy helps you inch your monthly debt obligation closer to that desirable 25 percent figure by enabling you to use more money per month to pay down higher-interest debts.

You can start by talking to your bank. For the best mortgage rates, however, you need to shop around. Personal finance websites also give mortgage rate information. And the Canada

Mortgage and Housing Corporation (CMHC), the Crown corporation that insures a number of mortgages in Canada, can help a lot in this particular area of finance.

Also, if refinancing your mortgage would free up enough money to help you, doing so is a much better deal than taking out a home equity loan, which carries an interest rate that is a couple of points higher than the current mortgage rate.

Even if you think you'll need a home equity loan too, refinance your mortgage before you consider the loan. You may be surprised at how much you save, and you may decide against the loan. Plus, it's harder to renegotiate your original mortgage when you have a second mortgage on the house.

Find more money

You can look in a number of places for extra money — not all are easy, but all are worth considering.

The first thing to do is to review your nonessential expenses (discussed in Chapter 1). Scrutinize anything not related to your survival — think cable TV, the weekly laser facial treatments, the super-deluxe gourmet coffee you pick up on the way to work each morning. Then cut out those items you can live without.

You may even want to review your essential expenses and decide whether you can get by with spending less. For example, you could move into a less expensive apartment and save money each month, or you could buy food and other essentials in bulk to cut your costs.

You may think these small things won't make much of a difference, but consider this: If you have a 30-year mortgage of $100,000 at 8 percent, adding just $1 — yup, one loonie — per day to your payment can save you $27,000 in interest and cut four years off the duration of the loan. These changes may look small, but they can have a huge effect in the long run.

The following sections list some specific places to look for money. For other ways (increasing deductibles on insurance, finding cheaper sources of clothes, and so on), see the section on borderline/debatable expenses in Chapter 1. When you get into the swing of things, you'll probably think of other areas in which you can cut back or other projects you can do to save or earn money.

Reduce essential variable expenses

Figuring out how to reduce essential variable expenses is one way that most people, even those who are not in debt, try to cut down on their monthly expenses. Getting good at this is useful even after you reach your goals.

- **Reduce your taxes.** Well, at least temporarily. If you normally get a refund from your income taxes, revisit your TD1 form (the form your employer uses to determine the correct amount of tax to withhold from your paycheques). Carefully go through the form to ensure that you are claiming all the exemptions you're entitled to. You may not get a refund next year, but your take-home pay will increase. Getting 12 monthly mini-refunds now rather than one big one next spring is much better, don't you agree?

- **Get out the scissors.** Start using coupons and shopping for bargains. (However, don't drive kilometres and kilometres to save a few cents on milk — you'll burn more in gas than you'll save.)

- **Eat up.** Never go to the grocery store hungry, because you'll tend to buy more than you intended.

- **Avoid brands.** Buy generic food and over-the-counter drugs.

- **Shop around for insurance rates.** Change automobile insurance companies, or raise your deductible, to get a lower monthly premium.

- **Layer, layer, layer.** Wear a sweater instead of turning up the heat, or open the windows instead of running the air conditioner. A few degrees of difference in temperature can make a significant difference in your heating and cooling bills (and consuming less energy is good for the planet).

- **Do it yourself.** Learn to do minor repairs and home maintenance jobs yourself.

- **Fix it.** Repair or mend items rather than replace them.
- **Use your feet.** Walk (or carpool, bike, or take public transportation) when possible to save money on gasoline.

Change your (expensive) habits

Your habits can have a huge effect on the outflow of money. Consider these examples:

- **If you smoke, quit.** A two-pack-a-day habit, at $10 a pack, translates into $7,300 per year.
- **Stop drinking.** As with smoking, what seems like a negligible amount of money adds up swiftly.
- **"Borrow" some savings.** Head to the public library rather than purchasing books at a bookstore. In addition to books, you can check out movies and music for free.
- **Take your lunch to work.** Dining even in an inexpensive restaurant can add a couple of dollars a day to your budget. Bring your own coffee, too, unless your company supplies it for free.
- **Adjust your movie-going habits.** Go to movies only during matinee hours or after they hit the discount theatres. You can also rent videos or borrow them from the library and have a family movie night at home.

Find miscellaneous money

You can look for, or earn, more money in a variety of other places:

- **Switch to an interest-bearing chequing account.** Even if you don't earn much in interest, any money you earn helps your situation.

- **Stop paying for chequing.** Look for a chequing account that requires a lower minimum balance for free chequing. If you switch from a bank that has a $1,500 minimum to one with a $1,000 minimum, you can instantly apply the $500 to paying off debts. Check out credit unions — they're great.

- **Hold a garage sale.** If you have items that are more valuable than the usual garage sale stuff, try selling them through the newspaper, by posting a note on the bulletin board at work, or on the Internet.

- **Get a part-time job.**

- **Tutor or consult in a field in which you excel.**

- **If you're doing good work, ask for a raise.**

- **Rethink your vacation.** Find out whether you can get vacation pay instead of taking time off. You don't want to do this with all your vacation time, because even folks who are broke need time off, but doing it for part of your vacation may help you along.

- **Rent out a spare room.**
- **Barter.** Find a friend or acquaintance who will babysit your kids in return for your mowing their lawn, or vice versa. Find someone who will fix your car in exchange for your cooking dinner. You get the idea. The possibilities are almost limitless.

Cut to the quick

If you've cut back everything else and you still can't make ends meet, you may have to do something about your essential expenses. Consider the following ideas:

- **If you have two cars, sell one.** Take public transportation or carpool. If you must have two cars, see whether you can downgrade — get a vehicle with lower payments.
- **Revisit your housing situation.** If your financial situation is really bad, consider selling your house and buying either a smaller house or a condo. Remember, it's better to sell your home than to have it taken away, because then you have nothing. This suggestion applies only if you have cut all nonessential expenses and still can't make your monthly payments.

- **Adjust your alimony payments.** If you're paying alimony or child support to a former spouse who is doing better than you are financially, you may be able to apply for a reduction in those payments.

Some of these measures may seem drastic, but they're not nearly as drastic, or as potentially damaging, as bankruptcy (which you can read more about later in this chapter). The measures in this section may inconvenience you, but they're not designed to destroy your credit history or seriously impair your lifestyle, as bankruptcy can.

Talk to your family

As a last resort, turn to your family for financial assistance. Do you have relatives who could lend you money to pay off your debts? Consider promising them a return on investment. For example, you could pay them 5 percent interest on the loan and still save a vast amount of money if the interest on your debts is high.

Of course, it's vital that you pay back these loans. Because you have an insider's view of what it's like to be strapped for cash, you certainly don't want to put anyone you care about in a similar position. Besides, it's almost impossible to overstate how important it is for your self-esteem, your sense of accomplishment, and the success of your long-term goals that you pay back all debts, including (and maybe especially) those owed to family.

A Look at Credit-Counselling Agencies

If your debt load is troubling you, consider contacting a not-for-profit credit-counselling agency. Two umbrella organizations can help you find an approved agency in your area:

- **Canadian Association of Credit Counselling Services:** 800-263-0260; info@financialfitness.ca; https://financialfitness.ca/
- **Credit Counselling Canada:** 866-398-5999; contact @creditcounsellingcanada.ca; www.credit counsellingcanada.ca

Some credit-counselling agencies are licenced by government departments, some are attached to Family Services departments, and some are independent. Their funding comes from a variety of different sources, including provincial governments, the United Way, local government, and creditors. Different offices have different funding arrangements.

The goal of nonprofit credit-counselling agencies is to offer no-cost (or low-cost) credit counselling. Depending on your situation, you may simply be given some ideas about how to manage your savings better and assistance in budgeting.

The agencies also put a strong emphasis on education to assist people in not continuing with debt-happy habits. A member organization can also contact creditors for you, set you up with a third-party mediator, or assist you in obtaining a consolidation loan.

Beware biased advice

One woman, whose family racked up significant debt due largely to unexpected expenses and a reduction in her income, found herself in trouble with too much debt. So she turned to a credit-counselling service, which she heard about through its advertising and marketing materials.

The credit-counselling agency she went to markets itself as a "nonprofit community service." The woman, like many others, found that the service was not objective. After her experience, the woman feels that a more appropriate name for the organization she worked with would be the Credit Card Collection Agency.

Unbeknownst to her — and many others — some credit-counselling agencies get their funding from the fees that creditors pay them. These credit-counselling agencies collect fees on a commission basis — just as collection agencies do! Their strategy is to place those who come in for help on their debt-management program. Under this program, counselees agree to pay a certain amount per month to the agency, which in turn parcels out the money to the various creditors.

Because of the woman's tremendous outstanding consumer debt (it exceeded her annual income), her repayment plan was doomed to failure. She managed to make ten months' worth of payments, largely because she raided a retirement account for $28,000. Had she filed bankruptcy (which she ultimately needed to do), she would have been able to keep her retirement money. But her counsellor never discussed the bankruptcy option. "I received no counselling," the woman says. "Real counsellors take the time to understand your situation and offer options. I was offered one solution: a forced payment plan."

Others who have consulted various credit-counselling agencies — including a research assistant who, undercover, visited an office to seek advice — confirm that some agencies use a cookie-cutter approach to dealing with debt. Such agencies typically recommend that debtors go on a repayment plan that has the consumer pay, say, 3 percent of each outstanding loan balance to the agency, which in turn pays the money to creditors.

Although such credit-counselling agencies' promotional materials and counsellors aren't shy about highlighting the drawbacks to bankruptcy, counsellors are reluctant to discuss the negative effect of signing up for a debt payment plan. The woman's counsellor never told her that restructuring her credit-card payments would tarnish her credit reports and scores. The counsellor who the researcher met with also neglected to mention this important fact. When asked, the counsellor was evasive about the debt-management program's effect on the researcher's credit report.

If you're considering bankruptcy or you're otherwise unable to meet your current debt obligations, first be sure to read the rest of this chapter. Also, interview any counselling agency you may be considering working with. Remember that you're the customer and you should do your homework first and be in control. Don't allow anyone or any agency to make you feel that they're in a position of power simply because of your financial troubles.

Ask questions and avoid debt-management programs

Probably the most important question to ask a credit-counselling agency is whether it offers *debt-management programs* (DMPs), whereby you're put on a repayment plan with your creditors and the agency gets a monthly fee for handling the payments. You do *not* want to work with an agency offering DMPs because of conflicts of interest. An agency can't offer objective advice about all your options for dealing with debt, including bankruptcy, if it has a financial incentive to put you on a DMP.

The Financial Consumer Agency of Canada provides safeguards and suggestions for you to consider before hiring a counselling agency (www.canada.ca/en/ financial-consumer-agency/services/ debt/debt-settlement-company.html). Following is an overview:

- **Watch out for high-pressure sales tactics.**
- **Beware of unrealistic promises.** Debt settlement companies cannot guarantee to reduce your debts by a large amount, to prevent creditors from trying to get back the money you owe in court, and to stop creditors' phone calls, among other actions.
- **Check the fees.** You may be charged advance fees, even if the company cannot get creditors to reduce your debt.
- **Research the company's reputation.** Check for complaints made to the Better Business Bureau (www.consumerhandbook.ca/en/contacts/ better-business-bureaus); l'Office de la protection du consommateur (Quebec) (www. opc.gouv.qc.ca/en/consumer/); and your provincial or territorial consumer affairs office (www.consumerhandbook.ca/en/contacts/ provincial-territorial-offices).
- **Review the contract.**

The Scoop on Bankruptcy

If you say "debt," most people immediately think "bankruptcy." Canada is facing an epidemic of personal bankruptcy. But bankruptcy is not an easy solution. It can seriously disrupt your life, it ruins your credit history, and it's possible it won't get rid of most of your debts. Make sure you know all the facts before you consider this dreadful option.

Your best bet: Avoid bankruptcy

If a chronic gambler deserts his wife and leaves her with a hefty mortgage, $90,000 in credit card debt, and six children, she might want to consider bankruptcy. For almost everyone else, bankruptcy is probably a bad choice. Here's why:

- You can lose much of your personal property. The court sells the property to pay your creditors. If you're going to lose everything anyway, why not sell it yourself? You'll probably get a better price for it, and you won't have a bankruptcy ruining your credit report.

- The blot remains on your credit record for six to seven years, so you probably won't be able to take out loans, get credit cards, or do anything else that requires a review of your credit record.

- If a friend or relative co-signed a loan, they are not protected by your bankruptcy and will have to repay your debts.

- Bankruptcy takes away the safety net of security that credit can supply your family.

- Bankruptcy hurts innocent people who trusted you to repay. It has a major effect on merchants and lenders and can, in the long run, mean job loss or business closure.

- You aren't likely to learn the necessary lessons to keep you from repeating your folly. In fact, a staggering 50 percent of the people who file bankruptcy file again later in their lives because they have changed no patterns and learned no new skills.

- You reveal your unfortunate financial lifestyle to the public in technicolour. Your bankruptcy petition, schedules, and payment plan are public documents. It's almost like having a tattoo on your forehead — especially in the business world.

- If you have a job that involves being bonded (bank teller, jewellery clerk), it may be in jeopardy.

- Bankruptcy is humiliating. It seriously undercuts your self-esteem and really makes it difficult for you to make positive changes in your life.

Many of these points apply only if your filing is successful, which is not necessarily guaranteed. If you fail to follow any of the necessary steps, such as showing up for the creditors' meeting, answering the court's questions honestly and completely, or producing the necessary and verifiable books and records, the case can be dismissed. If this happens, you still owe everything you did before you started, and you're out whatever you've spent so far on bankruptcy proceedings.

Today, too many people are filing for bankruptcy to escape debt that is merely inconvenient. The courts are getting stricter, and are looking more closely at all cases. Judges are diligently on the lookout for people who are simply trying to get out of paying their bills, as opposed to those who are truly suffering hardship. If a judge determines you have enough income to cover the monthly payments for your debts, and especially if you have any discretionary income left after making those payments, your bankruptcy case likely will be thrown out of court.

Dischargeable and nondischargeable debts

Not all debts go away when you file for bankruptcy. Most unsecured debts are *dischargeable,* which means you are no longer legally required to repay them. However, some unsecured debts are *nondischargeable* — that is, you still have to repay them even after filing for bankruptcy. For secured debts, you surrender the property you used as collateral, or pay the debt if you want to retain the collateral.

Which type of debt you have determines whether you have anything to gain from declaring bankruptcy:

- **Dischargeable debts** include, but are not limited to, credit card purchases, rent, and health care bills.

- **Nondischargeable debts** include, but are not limited to, student loans, alimony or child support, any debt or liability arising out of fraud or embezzlement, debts incurred as a result of criminal acts, and eve-of-bankruptcy spending sprees (or any substantial purchases close to the time of filing).

In addition, after you file for bankruptcy, your creditors have 45 days to object. If they file a suit, it's possible that a discharge will be denied for the debt in question.

You can't really guess what the judge will decide about your creditors' suits (unless you know one of your creditors is in worse shape financially than you are), but you should be able to identify your dischargeable debts. If most of your debts are dischargeable, bankruptcy can help reduce your debt burden — but don't forget, that doesn't mean it makes your problems go away.

Alternatives to bankruptcy

 Bankruptcy is a drastic move with serious long-term consequences. Consider these options first:

- **Talk to your creditors.** Hard as it may sound, you can call up your creditors and explain why you haven't made your payments. Ask for lower payments over a longer time frame. They may allow it.

- **Consider credit counselling.** Credit counselling services differ from province to province, but all of them can give sound advice on creating a budget and sticking to it. (Find out more about credit counselling previously in this chapter.)

- **Apply for a consolidation order.** If you live in British Columbia, Alberta, Saskatchewan, Nova Scotia, or P.E.I., you can apply for a consolidation order, which defines the amount and the times that you have to make payments to the court. The court will then pay your creditors. (In Quebec, a similar option is called a voluntary deposit.) With a consolidation order, you can pay off your debts over three years and you're free from wage garnishees and harassment from creditors. Plus, you get to keep your stuff.

- **Make a consumer proposal.** Under the Bankruptcy and Insolvency Act, you may make a proposal to your creditors to reduce the amount of your debts, extend the time to repay the debt, or provide some combination of both. (More on this is in the next section.)

If none of these methods solves your debt problem, you may want to consider bankruptcy.

The consumer proposal

As a last measure before declaring outright bankruptcy, you can make a consumer proposal to your creditors that you pay less each month over a longer period of time, or pay a certain percentage of what you owe. The main benefit is that your unsecured creditors cannot take legal steps to recover debts from you — such as seizing property or garnisheeing wages. You can make a consumer proposal if your debts total less than $250,000, not including a home mortgage.

The procedure begins when you seek the help of an administrator, who may be a trustee or someone appointed by the superintendent of bankruptcy. He or she will assess your finances, and give you advice about what kind of proposal may be best for you and your creditors. You'll have to sign the required forms, and the administrator will send the proposal — along with a report that lists your assets, debts, and creditors — to the official receiver, as well as to each of your creditors. The creditors then have 45 days to decide whether to accept or reject your proposal.

If your creditors accept your consumer proposal, they determine the amount and time periods by which you'll clear yourself of debt. If they reject it, just about the only option left is bankruptcy.

It will cost you money to make a consumer proposal: You have to pay a filing fee to the superintendent of bankruptcy, and the administrator will expect to be paid. The fees for administrators, however, are determined by law. You can check them out at the superintendent of bankruptcy's website at www. ic.gc.ca/eic/site/bsf-osb.nsf/eng/home.

How to tell whether bankruptcy is for you

Before you go to the trouble and expense of beginning bankruptcy proceedings, appraise your situation and determine if you have anything to gain from filing bankruptcy. Gather your debt worksheets and your budget, ask yourself the following questions, and think about what your answers may mean when you're considering bankruptcy. Be precise and realistic, because the trustee and court officials will be.

- **Do you have any discretionary income left after you make the minimum payments on all bills and cover all essential expenses?**

  If your answer is yes, forget bankruptcy. More than likely, your application will be dismissed.

  If your answer is no, go on to the next question.

- **Would a trustee be likely to view any items in your budget as nonessential?**

  If your answer is yes, you have two options. You can eliminate the item yourself and put the money toward your bills. Or, if the item is important to you, avoid bankruptcy so you can retain your option of spending that money.

  If your answer is no, go on to the next question.

- **Are you behind on payments of secured debts, such as mortgage and car payments?**

  If your answer is yes, contact the creditors and try to make arrangements to catch up on payments.

  If your answer is no, continue to pay your bills and budget carefully; you're probably not a good candidate for bankruptcy.

- **Compare all the debts on your debt worksheet to the list of nondischargeable debts earlier in this chapter. Is a considerable portion of your debt nondischargeable?**

If your answer is yes, you have little to gain from filing for bankruptcy.

If your answer is no, go on to the next question.

• **Do you have property you could sell (that is, without liens or other impediments) that would probably be taken from you if you filed for bankruptcy?**

If your answer is yes, you may want to sell it yourself, apply the money toward your bills, and keep your credit record clean.

If your answer is no — that is, either you have no property that could be taken away or liens exist on the property, so it couldn't be sold — bankruptcy may be an option.

• **Did a friend or relative co-sign any of the loans the bankruptcy would affect?**

If your answer is yes, talk to that individual to find out whether he or she is able to repay, because the debt will become that person's if you file for bankruptcy. If your friend or relative can repay, perhaps he or she can do so without having you file, and then you can repay that individual in time.

If your answer is no, continue looking into bankruptcy if you feel it's necessary.

Pretty much all the other considerations are personal or emotional. Are you comfortable with having officials establish your budget? Are you comfortable with the thought of having this mark against your credit history for years and being unable to get loans, credit cards, and so on? Do you lack the discipline to carry out a repayment plan without the threat of legal intervention? Are you willing to give up much of your property to creditors? Will you be able to recover emotionally from the process? Indeed, the bankruptcy process is about as much fun as an expensive root canal.

3

Mapping Your Habits

Whether you're in Montreal, Medicine Hat, or Mozambique, just about every map you come across will likely have a "You Are Here" arrow. Why? Because you can't get to where you want to be if you don't know where you are.

Your financial snapshot is a tool to help you map out and reach your financial goals, and it's useless unless you know where you are now and where you want to go. Determine your current financial situation by taking a thorough survey of your financial status. This chapter shows you how to track your spending habits and personality.

How to Figure Out What You Spend

In your financial life, you may spend (or pay bills) until you have no more money. Then you wait for your next paycheque and start the process all over again. That approach may have worked (although not all that well) back in the days when you were collecting an allowance from Mom and Dad. It may have worked even in university — at least you wouldn't freeze. As time goes on, though, this "system" becomes less and less sound.

This section helps you figure out where you are currently spending your money so you can lay the groundwork for wiser, more informed decisions about your spending.

Keep a spending diary

Keeping a spending diary helps you determine how you're spending your money on a day-to-day basis. For your diary, use a small notebook that fits in your pocket or purse. Carry it everywhere. Attach a pen or pencil to it so you have no excuse for not writing down every purchase you make. Every day. Every cent. (You can also use the notes app on your smartphone instead of a notebook.) Keep your spending diary for at least a month. Take a month off and start again, doing a month in each season.

On each new page, write the day and date. Record all your purchases, whether you spent cash, used a credit card, or added to a tab. At the end of each day, total your expenses. (To make this exercise even more useful and meaningful, divide your weekly after-tax income by seven, write that amount on each day's page, and at the end of the day figure out whether you spent more than you made that day.)

Try one of these three ways to keep your diary:

- **Basic:** Create just two columns — one for the amount and one for a description.

- **Detailed:** Decide how many categories you want, and then draw and label your columns (you'll probably want to use two facing pages). Categories may include groceries, restaurant meals, snacks, transportation, clothing, and telephone calls.

- **Obsessive:** Draw fewer columns for wider categories, such as food, transportation, utilities, clothes, and miscellaneous. Write a key in the front or back of your notebook so you can keep track of the items within each category. For example, under food you could use G for groceries, R for restaurant meals, S for snacks, and so on, as shown in Table 3-1.

  You will want to create your own key based on your lifestyle. In Table 3-1, for example, B may stand for bus fare, F for fuel, N for newspapers, and C for expensive specialty coffee (or clothing, if you're into that).

Food	Transportation	Miscellaneous
R $10.50	B $5.25	N $2.75
S $2.50	F $39.48	C $39.00
G $33.88		

Table 3-1: *Sample Daily Spending Diary*

If your miscellaneous column adds up too fast, you probably need more categories. And if you find that you're altering your spending habits as you keep your diary, don't write your totals until the end of the month.

Use other tools to track your spending

Your bank and credit card statements can help you keep a handle on your spending. Rather than just checking to make sure the amounts are correct, use these records to find out how much money you spend in each category you use in your spending diary.

Using the information you've gathered, you can use pencil and paper to create a financial worksheet. Or use financial software on a computer or handheld device to keep track of your spending and saving habits.

The time you invest now to gather information and understand your financial fingerprint will pay off in easier tracking and decision making later. You've already made the decisions about your money; now you just have to apply them.

Review your bank records

Every month, your bank, credit union, or other financial institution sends you a list of how much you put into your accounts and how much you spent out of them. Bank records are a good place to put your expenditures in categories using different-coloured highlighters: Try green for savings and red for impulse purchases.

Your banking can be remarkably slick if you have Internet access and use online banking. All Canadian banks have systems where you can see current and even past records online. You can find out whether a specific cheque has cleared. You can see your current balance. You can check your records when it's convenient for you rather than waiting for the post office to deliver your statement. In addition, you can make your financial tracking life easier by using your computer to set up automatic payments for such expenses as

- Mortgage
- Utilities
- Telephone
- Credit cards
- Savings
- Investments

The easier you make it to keep track of your finances, the more likely you are to do it.

Monitor your credit card statements

Those handy reports — or devastating reminders of how much you've spent and how much you owe, depending on your perspective — you get every month recording your credit card activity also help you draw your financial map. Tapping or inserting a card to make a purchase is so easy that many people do so much more often than they should. Again, using highlighters, mark each purchase to be tallied in a specific category.

Use financial management software

Computers can do many things for you. Luckily, keeping track of your money is one of them. Programs such as Quicken and Microsoft Money are inexpensive yet flexible. These programs do the basics, such as keeping track of your cheque record and balancing your chequebook. But that's just the beginning.

Like the worksheet in Table 3-2 later in this chapter, financial management software creates a budget for you according to your specifications. Even better than automatically calculating totals as you enter amounts, the software enables you to move items from category to category. (For example, you may want to move restaurant meals from a Food category to a Personal category — your choice.) This software enables you to be as specific or as imprecise as you want. You can create categories down to the nth degree, monitoring not only how much you spend in groceries but also how much of that you spent for meat, cereal, cookies, and ice cream — or whatever your idea of the four basic food groups may be.

Flexibility allows you to reorganize your budget so it gives you the information you want. When you've set up a budget, you aren't stuck with it. And as your situation changes, you can customize your budget to reflect your new reality.

With your software package, you can compare your forecast spending with your actual spending in any category, know when expenses are due, monitor your loan payments, manage your investments, and create reports and graphs to show how you're progressing toward your goals.

Don't put off budgeting because you don't have a computer. Software is nice, but not necessary. On the other hand, don't avoid using a computer or handheld device for budgeting simply because you're intimidated by them. You likely have a friend or family member who is comfortable with computers. (And any number of books can help you through most computer or handheld device issues you may have.)

Evaluate where your money goes

With your spending diary in hand, you have the information you need to set up your budget. Knowing where money goes can help you keep it from going.

Table 3-2 is a budgeting worksheet that shows you what your spending history looks like. Using the last six months of bank and credit card records, figure your expenses in each category. For items that fluctuate, such as food, add up your six-month total (SMT). Then double that amount to get your yearly cost. Divide your SMT by 2 for your quarterly cost for that item. Divide your SMT by 6 to determine your monthly cost. Divide your SMT by 26 to calculate your weekly cost. Prepare to be shocked at how much you're spending in some categories.

Expenses	Weekly	Monthly	Yearly
Housing			
Rent or mortgage			
Condo association dues			
Maintenance			
Property taxes			
Insurance			
Furniture and appliances			
Other housing expenses			
Utilities			
Gas			
Telephone			
Water			
Electricity			
Other utilities expenses			
Food			
Groceries			
Eating out			
Other food expenses			

Table 3-2: *Budgeting Worksheet*

Expenses	Weekly	Monthly	Yearly
Transportation			
Automobile lease/payment 1			
Automobile lease/payment 2			
Licensing			
Insurance			
Maintenance			
Gasoline			
Taxis and public transportation			
Parking/tolls			
Other transportation expenses			
Health			
Dentist(s)			
Eye care			
Prescriptions			
Insurance			
Other health expenses			
Education			
Tuition/school fees			
Books and supplies			
School activities			
Other education expenses			
Personal			
Clothing, shoes			
Haircuts			
Cosmetics			
Pet care			

(continued)

Expenses	Weekly	Monthly	Yearly
Childcare			
Child support (you pay out)			
Allowances			
Gifts			
Donations			
Membership dues			
Books and magazine and newspaper subscriptions			
Laundry/dry cleaning			
Hobbies			
Vacations			
Entertainment			
Other personal expenses			
Investments			
Savings accounts			
RRSP(s)			
TFSA(s)			
Mutual funds			
Bonds			
Other investment expenses			
Credit and loan			
Credit card 1			
Credit card 2			
Credit card 3			
Department store card			

Table 3-2: *(continued)*

Expenses	Weekly	Monthly	Yearly
Gasoline card			
Student loan			
Other credit and loan expenses			
TOTAL EXPENSES			
Income	**Weekly**	**Monthly**	**Yearly**
Wages, total			
Gratuities			
Royalties			
Dividends and interest			
Trust fund			
Pension			
CPP and EI			
Child support paid to you			
Gifts			
TOTAL INCOME			

Table 3-2: *(continued)*

With Table 3-2, you can know how much you're spending in each category. After you create a budget based on what you want to spend in each category and adjust your spending habits accordingly, you'll be able to tell when you overspend or underspend in a category. Neither situation is cause for despair or jubilation as long as your long-term expenditures stay within your personal range.

If you consistently overspend, you may need to cut costs, or you may have underestimated your costs initially. On the other hand, if you consistently underspend your allowance in any category, you may be able to lower that budget item and reallocate the difference.

How to Identify Your Money Personality

The best-laid plans are worthless if you can't follow them. To find the best plans for you, and to help you stick to your budget, you need to understand how you feel about money and how you react to money matters. This section describes a few of the most common money personality types.

 You need to understand not only your own money personality but also that of your spouse or partner. (As you teach your children about budgeting and saving, you'll need to identify their money personalities, too.) When you recognize your money personality type, you can identify what habits you need to keep or change to reach your financial goals.

You save for a rainy day

If your money personality is closest to a *saver*, you have trouble spending money even when doing so is in your best interests.

You may think that a saver wouldn't have any changes to make. But you can save to the point of hurting yourself. When going out of your way to save a few dollars or cents creates extra effort or inconvenience for you (or for your family or friends), you've likely spent where you could have saved. For example, if you hire a cube van to move a few heavy items, and rush to return it before a deadline so you can save a few dollars or get back a deposit, you may cause yourself and those who are helping you a few aches and pains (literally and figuratively).

You spend like there's no tomorrow

If you're a *spender,* your immediate reaction to available cash (or even available credit) is to figure out what you can buy with it. Sometimes you spend because you can't resist salespeople. Spenders use credit if they don't have cash, with no concern for the long-term consequences of that debt.

A spender has more problems to overcome than the obvious. The attitude that any money available is available only to spend rather than to put in saving, is its own problem. But it's not unbeatable. If you learn to stop, evaluate, consider alternatives, and make a decision instead of reacting to the desire to spend (or giving in to a sales pitch), you'll have a more secure financial future.

Millions of aging North Americans are only now realizing that their savings are inadequate relative to their future goals. The good news is that many of these people have also begun to quickly shift gears to spend less, save more, and retire well.

You spend on a whim

If you're an *impulse buyer,* your spending habits are a little different from plain old spenders. When you see something you like, you buy it without evaluating the purchase in terms of your long-range goals. Impulse buyers react to one or two types of items (whereas spenders buy everything).

An impulse buyer is similar to a spender. But an impulse buyer doesn't even have to find money available for spending. Just seeing something to buy is enough to bring out the wallet or credit card. The desirable habit to cultivate is the same as that for a spender. If you figure how many hours of after-tax income would be needed to buy an item, you can stop much of your impulse buying in its tracks. If you have a working sound system, for example, is it really worth hundreds of work hours to replace it with a new one?

You take your time on a purchase

The last category is the *cautious buyer.* If this is your money personality, you are a serious comparison shopper who may waste more time making a decision than the item is worth.

Cautious buyers may waste both time and money. But time is money. Not only may a cautious buyer spend too much time gathering information about various features and comparing prices, but there's also the cost of phone calls and driving around. Even worse, a cautious buyer may not enjoy a purchase after making it if he or she sees the item on sale later.

If you're a cautious buyer, use those good comparison-buying skills but learn when enough information is enough to make a decision and ignore any information you gather after the purchase.

 If you have a lot of trouble making a buying decision, you may not need to buy that item at all.

4

Needs versus Wants

One of the responsibilities of being an effective money manager is to look at your financial situation objectively. Your objective eye lets you step back from the transactions you have conducted in the past and encourages you to look at the bigger picture of your financial situation. In practice, of course, this self-assessment process is easier said than done. But to help you stay disciplined, this chapter provides guidance as you fully consider what your needs and wants really are.

Look at the habits and attitudes you have developed up to now toward managing, spending, and saving money. Have you made good choices thus far for your hard-earned money?

Making good choices involves distinguishing what you need now and in the longer term from what you only wish you had now.

What I Really Need

What are the necessities of life, and how do these necessities change over time? Certainly, what you thought you needed at age 5 (a bike, a grilled cheese sandwich) would not be on your list of perceived needs when you were 15 (designer shoes, a new video game, a meal at the mall) or 25 (a new suit, a trip to Hawaii, money to pay the rent or mortgage, a romantic dinner on the town).

Start with the basics: You need housing, food, clothing, and some form of transportation to get to and from your job and other important places. But the range of choices for addressing those basic needs is staggering. Your cost, in terms of both money and opportunity, will vary greatly depending on your financial goals and the choices you make.

An *opportunity cost* is something you have to give up to pursue a particular decision. For example, if you decide to work late one evening, your opportunity cost involves giving up dinner with your family. If you decide to go to graduate school, your opportunity cost involves forgoing a higher standard of living in the immediate future in hopes of bettering your opportunities later in life.

Housing

Your housing choices may include living at home, renting an apartment, sharing an apartment or home with roommates, or buying your own place. For the sake of example, plug in some numbers for each of these options:

- If you rent a studio or one-bedroom apartment, your rent might run $1,800 a month.

- If you share an apartment or home with other roommates, your fair share might be $900 a month.

- If you buy your own house or condo, you might have to save $15,000 to $20,000 (at least) for a down payment, and your monthly mortgage might be $1,900 a month.

- If you take in a roommate or boarder to share your housing costs, or you take a smaller apartment or buy a smaller house, you can reduce your housing costs.

Your choice of housing depends on what you think you can afford as well as what you perceive the opportunity costs to be. Use Table 4-1 to apply the opportunity-cost concept to each housing choice, using figures that seem realistic for each choice listed.

Your perception of the benefits derived from each choice is just as important as the opportunity cost. By adding a fourth column to Table 4-1, you can identify what you think the benefits for each choice are.

Choice	Money Cost	Opportunity Cost	Benefits
Rent an apartment			
Share housing with roommate(s)			
Buy a condo or house			
Take in a boarder			
Downsize housing			
Other			

Table 4-1: *Monthly Housing Costs and Benefits*

What did you identify as the opportunity costs for sharing housing with roommates? Chances are, you mentioned a loss of independence. The opportunity costs associated with the other choices may involve settling for less in terms of the other major expenses in your life. For example, if you choose to rent a fancy apartment, you may have less to spend on a car. The choices you make for the basics depend on what you consider important to achieve the goals you identify in Chapter 5.

Food

Do you have any idea how much you spend on food each week or month? Are you counting fast-food stops and going to restaurants? Although food is certainly a necessity, you probably shouldn't count restaurant food as a necessity. Dining in a restaurant is usually considered entertainment. Eating out is something you want or enjoy more than something you need.

Use Table 4-2 before making decisions about the money you spend on food. Identify the opportunity costs and benefits for each of your options.

Food Choices	% of Total Expenses	Opportunity Cost	Benefits
Breakfast out			
Lunch out			
Dinner out			
Weekly groceries			
Other			

Table 4-2: *Monthly Food Costs and Benefits*

Sorting out your food choices and weighing the opportunity costs and benefits will help you make better money management decisions. You can discover how unwise it is to spend 40 percent of your net income on food when you also need to include in your budget costs for transportation and clothing. And you haven't even introduced all those things you want and are tempted to consider necessities, such as monthly cable, cellphone, and Internet access fees.

Transportation

In the category of transportation, too, you have a wide range of choices. Take a look at the choices you've made in the past to get a better idea of your money management patterns. Then fill in Table 4-3.

Transportation	% of Total Expenses	Opportunity Cost	Benefits
Car purchase payments			
Car lease payments			
Gasoline			
Insurance			
Maintenance, repairs, and so on			
Public transportation			
Other			

Table 4-3: *Monthly Transportation Costs and Benefits*

You already know that owning or leasing a vehicle is the most expensive form of transportation. And within the arena of owning a vehicle — car, minivan, sport utility vehicle, or motorcycle — many choices test your money management skills. You may want the best but find you can't afford all you want. This is where the critical skill of distinguishing between your economic needs and wants is crucial.

You may decide you need a car. The car you choose can range from a top-of-the-line model with payments of $925 a month for five years to a clunker for less than $1,000 total (all before factoring in repair costs). Your choice relates to your financial goals and the economic means, or income, at your disposal.

Clothing

Clothing costs are perhaps harder to deal with. People generally don't spend a fixed amount on clothes each month. However, a major clothing purchase, such as a coat, could cause a big bubble in a monthly budget if you don't have good money management skills.

The choice in clothing is enormous. You have a sliding scale from designer labels to resale shops. You may love to shop for clothes, or you may hate to. Try to separate your love (or hate) for clothes shopping from the opportunity costs and the benefits-specific clothes items.

Try to review your clothing costs for the last year. Begin by recalling major purchases. Estimate the number of times you go into a clothing store every week or month. Guess at how much you spend each time you make a purchase. The money you spend on clothes is probably greater than you think.

Add it up

Using Tables 4-1, 4-2, and 4-3 and your clothing estimate, tally the amounts you currently spend each month on the basics — housing, food, transportation, and clothing. Begin to think about the adjustments you want to make in any of those categories to accommodate greater spending (or savings) for any of your necessities. For instance, if buying a home is one of your priorities, you can anticipate paying a greater amount for the "necessity" of housing. A greater commitment to your housing expense may well require spending less in another area of your budget.

What I Really Want

One of the biggest differences between being an adult and being an adolescent is the amount of money you have available for discretionary spending. When you were a teenager, chances are your parents paid for your housing, food, and transportation. The money you earned, you spent — unless your parents insisted that you save some or trained you in money management skills.

So fast-food, video games, movies, fashionable clothing, and entertainment tickets often become the necessities of adolescents. Any survey of teenagers will likely indicate that their top expenses are for entertainment, clothing, and music, not necessarily in that order. But for adults, these items fall into the category known as discretionary spending.

The concept of discretionary spending

Thinking of all the things you want outside the basic necessities as *extras* may be hard to do, but in the world of personal finance, that's reality. Take this opportunity for a reality check so you can recognize the distinction between what you need (necessities) and what you want (extras).

As your own money manager, you may wish you had more money available for discretionary spending. And you may be appalled at which goods and services are commonly relegated to the category of extras. Look over the following checklist of items that you may consider ordinary parts of living. Indicate whether you think an item is a basic need (N) or a discretionary want (W).

_____ Stockpot	_____ Pet
_____ Manicure	_____ Beer
_____ Down comforter	_____ Books
_____ Television	_____ Movie tickets
_____ Internet access	_____ Bread
_____ Vacation in Florida	_____ Videos
_____ Washing machine	_____ Stove
_____ Dishwasher	_____ Wallet
_____ Haircut	_____ Acupuncture
_____ Cologne	_____ Sweater

Count up your Ns and Ws. The list of wants should be far greater than the list of needs. Your needs list might include haircut, bread, and sweater. Some people would argue that a wallet is a necessity; others may disagree. Still, only about 25 percent of these items can be considered real necessities.

The extras in your life far exceed your needs. One of the most difficult skills you have to learn as a money manager is how to say no to yourself.

The influence of advertising

One of the reasons you may have a hard time distinguishing between economic needs and wants is that advertisements are so persuasive. You're bombarded with advertising on the radio, on television, on the Internet, in the print media, and on billboards and buses.

One of your jobs as an adult is to liberate yourself from the compelling persuasions of creative advertising. One way to do so is to ask yourself a fundamental question: "Do I really need this (whatever it is)?" When you identify something as a want rather than a need, you gain control over the choice of whether to buy it.

How to Make Good Choices

Making good decisions about your hard-earned money is a skill you can build while playing the game of DICE. No, you're not going to gamble with your money; DICE is an acronym for

- **Distinguish** between needs and wants.
- **Identify** the opportunity costs and benefits associated with each of your choices.
- **Choose** an item based on your priorities, not on impulse.
- **Evaluate** your well-chosen purchase as a gift to yourself.

In the beginning, you may make some unwise choices. But as you gain experience as a money manager, your judgment will improve if you use the DICE approach.

Distinguish between needs and wants

As discussed in the earlier section "What I Really Want," get in the habit of distinguishing between what you need and what you want. Society encourages you to think that things you wish for are really things you need. Declare your independence and start making those judgments for yourself.

Your needs relate to the list of goals you develop in Chapter 5. Which of the following do you consider needs as opposed to wants?

____ Housing	____ Food	____ Transportation
____ Taxes	____ Insurance	____ Savings
____ Clothing	____ Utilities	____ Self-improvement

Chances are you consider all these categories essential to your financial success and your economic goals. Financial success is a result of the proper ordering of needs and wants, and allocating personal resources accordingly. For example, food is an essential item in every budget. Good money managers curtail the amount of money they spend on this item to save for other priorities.

What would you add to your list of essentials? Try limiting your list of essentials to ten items. These will become your priority list for later use.

Keep in mind that within each category in your list of essentials you have a multitude of choices. But limit the range to three: basic, middle of the road, and luxury. To help you accomplish your financial goals, after each of your essential items, identify whether you want the basic, middle, or luxury choice.

Identify opportunity costs and benefits

When you make decisions about spending your money to provide for the essentials on your list, keep in mind the worksheets on housing, food, and transportation (Tables 4-1, 4-2, and 4-3) that helped you identify your options. For each option, you can name the opportunity cost — what you will give up to pursue a given option — and the benefit — what you will gain when you select that option.

All these steps may seem clumsy at first, but soon they'll become habit and you'll find yourself gaining both speed and confidence in identifying the relative benefits and costs of the choices you have. Weighing the relative costs and benefits enhances your skills as a money manager.

Choose what's best for you

Knowing what's best can seem difficult or confusing. That's why having your list of priorities close at hand is worthwhile. In Chapter 5, you have the opportunity to write down long-term Goal A, five-year Goal B, and one-year Goal C. Here, make a list of your ten most essential economic needs. Next to each category on this list, write B for Basic, M for Middle of the Road, or L for Luxury to indicate what you think you will be able to afford. Put this list on the refrigerator.

Refer to these lists whenever you must make a decision about your essential economic needs. Obviously, choosing what's best for you involves selecting the option that's most in line with your stated goals.

Only you know your financial goals and economic priorities. Only you can make money management decisions that will help you achieve your personal goals.

Evaluate your choices

The way to continue making good money choices is to review your choices in terms of how they further your financial goals. Reward positive behaviour. Learn from the mistakes of poor choices as well. Both kinds of choices can develop your skills as a money manager.

 Following are a few ways to reward yourself for using sound money management:

- Pat yourself on the back by doing something you enjoy — take a walk, enjoy a hot bath, spend some time in your garden, or sign up for an inexpensive art, cooking, or dance class.

- Share the good news — tell a friend or family member about your choice and why it feels good in terms of your priorities.

- Make a donation to a charitable organization or cause you support. Keep receipts of these donations so that if you itemize on your tax return, you can take a deduction.

- Follow the DICE approach for another major purchase and feel good about how much better you are becoming at making wise choices.

5

Setting Financial Goals

Managing your money is a skill to be cultivated, just like developing your softball pitch or honing your fluency in a foreign language. As with any other skill, money management takes practice, realistic expectations, and the example and advice of those who have "been there and done that." This chapter is about setting realistic expectations for your personal finances, and then translating those goals into realistic actions.

Your Goals: Then and Now

Graduating from high school or university may have been your most important goal in the past. Or maybe your biggest goal was to land a new job or get back on your feet after a divorce. Perhaps you've achieved those goals and haven't really given much thought to what comes next. Perhaps you have a vague sense that you want to pay off your debts, start a family, put your children through college or university, or start your own business. None of these or any other goals will happen unless you make them happen.

Achieving financial success isn't a matter of luck. Financial success requires attention, discipline, and sound money management.

Setting financial goals is something like going grocery shopping. You go to the store with a sense of what you need or want to buy. But the number of choices, sales, and attractive displays may cause you to get sidetracked.

You're starting with the desire to manage your money successfully so you can achieve your financial goals. But getting distracted is easy. Just as a shopping list helps a shopper stay focused, a money management list can help you get off to a good start.

Take a minute to check off the items on the following money management "shopping list" that seem important to you. This shopping list can help you figure out your financial goals:

- Spend less than I make.
- Make good consumer choices, and get good value for money spent.

- Establish a good credit rating.
- Curb my spending appetite.
- Save some money every time I get paid.
- Spend enough time on money management.
- Take personal responsibility for managing my money.
- Work out a budget.
- Balance my chequebook.
- Know where to get good financial advice.
- Distinguish between short-term and long-term financial goals.
- Keep good records.
- Use banking services.
- Pay my bills and taxes on time.
- Eliminate my debt.
- Reduce my taxes.
- Plan my estate.

How many items apply to you? Chances are you think you need to do *all* these things. And you do. But you don't need to do everything at once. What you need to do first are the basics. The basic approach to managing your money starts with knowing your financial goals.

In general, your goal is probably financial security. The trouble comes in defining just what financial security means to you. Start right now and complete this sentence: *I will be financially secure when I . . .*

You may define financial security as being able to retire at age 65 without worrying about having enough money to live the rest of your life the way you want to. Or you may define financial security as being able to retire at age 50. The definition is up to you.

To get started on the road to financial security, begin to think in terms of the next five years. What can you do in the next five years that will help you accomplish your long-range goal of financial security?

Your Goals: A Five-Year Plan

Sound money management is achieved through simple, realistic goals. After you have determined your personal financial goals, classify those goals as short-term or long-term. Making this distinction is important because it provides your financial strategy with direction. When you have your short-term, midterm, and long-term goals clearly in mind, your goals become like building blocks. You can more easily defer some of the things you hope to accomplish in the short run because you know that those things will happen with a longer time frame.

To help sort out your goals, ask yourself where you want to be financially in five years. In Table 5-1, indicate which of the following goals are important for you to accomplish within the next five years. On a scale of 1 to 5, 5 is very important and 1 isn't very important.

Goal	[1]	[2]	[3]	[4]	[5]
Reduce debt	[ ]	[ ]	[ ]	[ ]	[ ]
Save money	[ ]	[ ]	[ ]	[ ]	[ ]
Buy a car	[ ]	[ ]	[ ]	[ ]	[ ]
Buy a home	[ ]	[ ]	[ ]	[ ]	[ ]
Start an investment program	[ ]	[ ]	[ ]	[ ]	[ ]
Reduce income taxes	[ ]	[ ]	[ ]	[ ]	[ ]
Buy life insurance	[ ]	[ ]	[ ]	[ ]	[ ]
Take an expensive vacation	[ ]	[ ]	[ ]	[ ]	[ ]
Put kids through university	[ ]	[ ]	[ ]	[ ]	[ ]
Other	[ ]	[ ]	[ ]	[ ]	[ ]
Other	[ ]	[ ]	[ ]	[ ]	[ ]

Table 5-1: *Five-Year-Goal Worksheet*

Look at the items you checked in the "5" column. Do you think it's realistic to try to accomplish all your 5's in the next five years? What do you think you can do in one year? The answers to these questions will help you focus on the important aspects of managing your money.

How to Set Priorities

Wanting it all is easy — who doesn't want a nice place to live, clothes with logos and labels, a great car, meals at romantic restaurants, vacations, and so on? The list expands so easily. The fact is that you have limited resources. You must work with what you have — not with what you want to have, and not with what you think you will get next month or next year.

All managers wish for more resources to accomplish their goals. All managers wish they had more time, more money, more people, and more experience. But effective managers are resourceful and use what they have to get the best results. They prove their skills by accomplishing tasks with discipline and motivation — skills you can develop when you approach money management with the commitment to making do with the money you have.

Manage your money to accomplish your goals

Take another look at your five-year-goal worksheet in Table 5-1. If you selected debt reduction as a very important goal, you'll probably decide on money strategies that will make that goal happen. If you selected both reducing your debts and buying a great car, your money strategies will have to be different. In fact, you may realize that your resources don't allow you to do both at the same time. One objective will have to take priority over the other.

From Table 5-1, select the three items you identified as most important to your short-term and long-term financial goals. Now rank those three objectives in their order of importance, as shown in Table 5-2.

Priorities	Short-Term	Mid-Term	Long-Term
1.			
2.			
3.			

Table 5-2: *Ranking My Priorities*

Do you think you need or want to make any adjustments to your worksheet? Chapter 4 examines the difference between money needs and money wants in greater detail. For now, stick with what you think you need to accomplish short term and long term.

Now estimate the percentage of your income you'll probably have to allocate to each of your top three priorities. Does common sense tell you these percentages are realistic? Pay attention to your common sense; it can become your best friend.

Write down what you know or expect your annual income will be this year before and after taxes and deductions.

Your *gross income* is your earnings before taxes and deductions get taken out of your paycheque. Your *net income* is your take-home pay — your earnings after all taxes and deductions. Your net income may seem like a lot of money or a pathetically small amount. In either case, as the manager of your money, you start with this amount.

Manage your time

Like the adage says, "Time is money." Deadlines are a fact of both personal and professional life. As the manager of your money, you will struggle with many of the same constraints business managers experience. On the one hand, you'll wish you had more time to accomplish your goals; on the other, you'll wish you could see and enjoy the results of your work sooner.

To become a successful money manager, you have to become a successful time manager as well.

Everybody has the same 24 hours in each of the 7 days of the week. Yet some people just seem to get more done than others do. Why? Because they have clear goals, good time management skills, commitment, and discipline. You, too, can put time management and money management skills to work to accomplish your financial goals.

Do a quick review of your typical week. Estimate the time you spend working, sleeping, eating, travelling, reading, watching television, shopping, dating, interacting with family, and playing. Which activity takes the most of your time? Is that activity really the top priority in your life? Setting your work aside for a moment, how much time have you set aside for the things that will help you achieve your financial goals? What time do you have for managing your money so your priorities can become a reality?

 Take the initiative to set aside half an hour every week (a weekend afternoon may be good, but find a time that works best for you) to develop your skills as an effective manager of your money and time. Time is undoubtedly one of your most valuable resources.

You can spend that half-hour doing any number of things. Consider the following:

- Make a list of your goals for the week.
- Review your out-of-pocket expenses against your budget.
- Read an article on personal finance.
- Call your financial adviser, trusted friend, or parent and ask for advice about a purchase or financial decision you expect to make in the coming week.

- Evaluate your money management skills during the past week and give yourself a grade. Target one area for improvement.

- Evaluate your time management skills during the past week and give yourself a grade. Target one area for improvement.

- Set aside $5 to $25 in an envelope for a special occasion.

- Identify at least one thing you believe you accomplished as a money and time manager during the past week.

- Start a weekly paper or electronic journal and enter a short list of your goals and accomplishments for the week.

- Compare your goals for the week against the priorities you set for yourself on the worksheet earlier in this chapter. Make adjustments.

Strategies for Success

Some experts think that setting financial goals is the easy part of money management. The hard part is making it happen. The high-level plans you make to accomplish your goals are called *strategies*. The thing about strategies is that you can change them.

Your plans or strategies for successful money management can change if you find that they aren't accomplishing their purpose. Just as a business manager has to make adjustments to respond to one problem or challenge after another, you can become skillful in making adjustments to manage your money more effectively.

Although many strategies are available to you as a money manager, at least two guidelines can help you evaluate the success of a strategy:

- Be flexible but focused.
- Learn to live on less.

Be flexible but focused

As a money manager, you want to develop a balance between keeping your goals clearly in mind and responding creatively and constructively to changing circumstances and unforeseen situations. No one can anticipate every circumstance in life. Just when you think you can save a little more during one month, the car needs a repair you didn't count on. Or perhaps you see an ad in the paper for an item you really need. Although you hadn't planned to make the purchase now, you think that buying it now will save money in the long run.

One of the best qualities of successful managers is good judgment. This is especially true of good money managers. Good judgment relates to common sense. Good judgment and common sense are not part of the school curriculum; you develop these in your life experiences.

Learning from your mistakes can be costly, but it's usually effective. Don't be afraid to change and try something else if one of your money management strategies isn't working.

 Often, you learn good judgment by the example of others you know and respect. Encourage others to share their stories with you. From their stories about the decisions they've made, you'll learn about the good sense to be flexible. You'll learn the balance of keeping your eye on your goals while making adjustments for setbacks or unexpected difficulties.

Find the level of risk you're comfortable with. If you don't have family responsibilities, taking greater risks may be easier. Taking the risk of changing jobs is easier if you're single than if you provide for a family. Some people find investing in a speculative stock easier than others. Know yourself and your financial obligations.

 Know that your goals may change as your circumstances change. Be flexible and replace goals that no longer suit your needs and wants. Your strategies may change because of proven successes and failures. Be flexible and make the necessary adjustments. If this approach sounds too vague to be useful now, test it by asking someone whose judgment seems sound and whose decisions you respect. Ask that person, "Am I being too rigid about (name a goal, strategy, or specific circumstance)?" Or ask, "How can I be more flexible about (name the specific situation)?"

Learn to live on less

The single most important skill you can develop as a money manager is to live below your means. You've probably heard this guideline — the key to your financial freedom — expressed in many different ways: Live on less. Put something away from every paycheque. Save for a rainy day. All too many people avoid heeding this important advice.

In the earlier section "Manage your money to accomplish your goals," you may have written down your net annual income. Try to imagine living on 90 percent of that income. Calculate how much you would need to save every month and every year to live on 90 percent of your net income. Think of a business manager who suddenly finds out that the budget for a particular project has been cut by 25 percent. The project still must be completed on time and with the same quality standards. As your own money manager, you can appreciate the flexibility and commitment to your goal that such adjustments require.

Investing allows your money to grow and is a reliable way to accomplish the ultimate goal of financial security. But if you don't manage to save money on a regular basis, you won't have money to invest. The way to save money regularly is to live below your means. The logic is simple and compelling.

Put aside for the moment the wish to own that boat or fancy car. Now is the time to face reality and develop the skills you need to manage your money well enough to accomplish your financial goals.

Your Goals: A, B, and C

Chapter 4 focuses on making good choices about spending. Before you make those choices, however, you need to take the time to nail down some strategies:

- **Review your five-year plan.** On a blank sheet of paper, write down what you consider your most important long-term goal. This is what you hope to accomplish in about five years. Label that Goal A.

- **Look ahead a few years.** Write down what you consider your most important financial goal for the next two to five years. This is your mid-term goal. Label that Goal B.

- **Focus on this year's achievement.** Write down your most important financial goal for this year. This is your short-term goal. Label that Goal C.

- **Re-evaluate your long-term goals.** Take another look at your five-year-goal worksheet in Table 5-1. After each item, write A, B, or C if the item relates to any of your specific financial goals.

- **Summarize your strategies.** Make a chart that lists your short-term goal and the money management strategies that will help you accomplish that goal. Do the same for your mid-term goal and related strategies, and your long-term goal and strategies.

- **Track your progress.** Put your chart of A, B, and C goals and strategies on the refrigerator door so you're reminded of them every day.

Think now about the annual increase you can realistically expect if you stay with the same job for the next five years. These increases may seem large or small to you. In a way, the size of the increases doesn't matter. What does matter is that you accept the realities of your situation and manage your money accordingly.

If you postpone major expenditures (such as the purchase of a new car or an expensive vacation) now to accomplish your most important objectives, will you realistically be able to afford those expenses later, given the revenue you expect? Begin to think of adjustments you need or want to make in your expectations.

6

Budgeting and Record Keeping

Pulling together all your financial information and building a budget aren't that hard. The challenge comes when you try to stick to that budget. Suddenly, you realize keeping to your reduced clothing or food allowance is tough. This chapter gives you the tools to help you stay within your budget. (See Chapter 2 for an introduction to budgeting.)

Your Essential Expenses: What You Need

Essential fixed expenses are those obligations you must pay regularly — usually monthly. Essential fixed expenses are the same month after month.

Although most people don't consider charitable contributions to be essential expenses, you can put those items in the essential category if they are important to you and you want to pay them regularly.

Essential variable expenses are due every month, but the amounts vary from month to month: food, gas, electricity, and so on. In this category, you prorate (average) regular expenses to a monthly cost. Do so by figuring your yearly cost and dividing by 12 (if you're using a monthly budget) or 52 (if you're using a weekly budget).

Essential fixed expenses include the following:

- Insurance that you pay monthly, quarterly, semi-annually, or annually
- Mortgage payment or rent
- Automobile payment
- Student loan payment

Essential variable expenses include the following:

- Groceries
- Utilities (gas, electricity, water, and so on)
- Public transit fares
- Gasoline
- Auto repairs and maintenance
- Health care and pharmaceuticals
- Haircuts, toiletries, and other personal care items
- Education and professional development costs (for your children or yourself)
- Savings for retirement
- Savings for large expenses, such as furniture, appliances, and replacement automobiles

As you update your budget, you'll remove items such as student loans as you pay them off.

Your Nonessential Expenses: What You Want

After you pay your essential expenses, what you have left is your *discretionary income*. From that, you pay your nonessential expenses (and put the rest in savings and investments).

Nonessential expenses include the following:

- Books, magazines, and newspaper subscriptions
- Restaurant meals
- Movies and concerts
- Gifts
- Vacations
- Hobbies

Chapter 3 lists various *money personalities* that identify how you feel about money and spending. Recognizing your money personality — and the money personalities of family members — helps you make better decisions about the money you've identified as nonessential spending.

In creating your budget, you're looking toward the future. You want to determine which items you listed as fixed expenses really should be considered nonessential. You may be shocked at the total of these items, but don't be discouraged.

The point of a budget is to have a plan for your money before you spend it. Without a budget, you can leave the house with $200 in cash, come back five hours later, and be able to account for only half that amount. With a budget, you'll never do that again. More importantly, you'll be able to make firm spending decisions based on criteria you have already set for yourself.

Hidden Expenses

Hidden expenses are those sneaky money-eaters that lurk everywhere. Knowing what and where they are and how much they cost helps you cut them by avoiding the items to which they are attached. This section identifies these hidden costs.

Bank machine, bank, and credit card fees

Hidden costs can quickly transfer your money from your pocket to an institution's profit statement. Be careful of the following:

- Annual fees
- Below-minimum use and below-minimum balance fees
- High interest rates
- Late-payment penalties
- Independent (or white label) ATMs (automated teller machines) not affiliated with any financial institution that charge fees of up to $3 for cash withdrawals
- Per-use fees

 Read all "change of terms" inserts you receive from banks, credit unions, credit card companies, and the like. The information they contain may be a wake-up call to change how and where you do business.

Not knowing what fees you're liable for with your money-handling institutions is the same as using a credit card without knowing what rate of interest you're paying. If you don't carry a balance on your credit card, the interest rate is irrelevant. If you don't incur fees from your bank and so on, you don't care what that rate is, either. But you need to know what and how much they are so you know what to do to avoid them.

Gratuities and delivery charges

The more services you use in your lifestyle, the more you pay in gratuities and delivery charges. Having meals or groceries delivered is convenient and may save you time, but in addition to paying for what you eat, you pay delivery costs and a tip to the delivery person — neither of which you can have for dessert.

Catalogue and Internet shopping can save a lot of time, along with parking and car-use costs. An add-on cost, however, may be shipping charges (often unrecoverable if you return the item). You may need to pay insurance costs as well, to protect against the item getting lost or damaged in transit. Plus, when you buy something in a store, you can inspect it before you take it home. And you can watch for sales.

This doesn't mean you should always shop in stores; it just means you need to know and compare the costs of various ways of taking care of your needs. If you use the time you save to earn more income, for example, the convenience may be worth the cost.

Sales, luxury, and utility taxes

Not all items are taxed at the same rate. Basic groceries, for example, are not taxed anywhere in Canada, but snacks (basically anything that can be eaten in one sitting) are, in some jurisdictions.

Governments have determined some items as luxury items. Liquor is a common example. In some places, the tax on a soft drink is lower than the tax on a beer — even though most people drink either one or both. The choices you make in what may seem to be the same category can lower these hidden costs. Read your receipts carefully. These days, most cash registers put added taxes, such as those for liquor, next to the item purchased so you can readily see how much you're paying for items for which substitutes may be available.

 Choosing one item over another may not save you a ton of money, but making saving decisions over and over can help put you on the path to financial security.

How to Factor in Emergency Expenses

You don't want to panic every time the refrigerator breaks down or the dog eats spoiled food and has to go to the vet. The budget you'll create later in this chapter reflects that emergencies do happen, so you'll have the savings put aside to pay for such contingencies.

You can move some items from the emergency category to a "savings for replacement" category by keeping track of those budget items. For example, one of the biggest money-eaters in the emergency category can be your automobile, especially if it isn't maintained properly and regularly.

Table 6-1 can help you keep track of your car's care and feeding. List all repairs, regular service (whether done at a service station or by you), and tire purchases. Review your car's service manual to be certain you're following the manufacturer's recommendations. A little short-term pain in the form of upfront maintenance expense usually goes a long way toward long-term gain in the form of extending your vehicle's life.

When deciding which auto parts to buy, the existence of a warranty and its terms can be deciding factors. Keeping track of the life of the warranty helps you get your dollar's worth. If a shop wants to add chargeable parts or labour to those covered by the warranty, push back hard by asking to see what needs to be replaced and why.

Date	Odometer Reading	Repair Description	Repair Warranty	Cost	Date Last Done

Table 6-1: *Automobile Maintenance: Major Repairs*

Some warranties are *prorated* (the cost for wear and tear is deducted), and others offer *replacements* (you get a new tire or other part). Knowing what you're buying makes comparison shopping easier.

Keep similar records on major appliances and furniture. Table 6-2 shows you what information you need to plan replacement purchases.

Now that you have an idea of how much money you should keep in an account to be able to pay cash for these items as you need them, you can put these amounts in your budget. Although you may choose to save the money for these items in your emergency fund, we suggest that you set up a household expenses fund to cover them.

Item	Date Purchased	Warranty Length	Expected Life	Purchase Price	Replacement Cost	Expected Replacement Date
Central air conditioner						
Clothes dryer						
Clothes washer						
Computer equipment						
Dishwasher						
Furnace						
Garage door opener						
Lawn mower						
Microwave						
Refrigerator						
Sofa						
Sound system						
Stove						
Sump pump						
Television						
Vacuum cleaner						
Water heater						
Other						
Other						
Other						

Table 6-2: *Major Purchases/Replacement Needs*

Talk about Taxes

Most people have their taxes deducted from their paycheques and don't need to deal with them separately until they file their tax returns. As your investment plans bring in more dividends and income, or if you take on another job that doesn't deduct taxes — for example, a freelance or contract job — be sure to review your tax withholdings and adjust them as needed. Doing so prevents a big tax bill at the end of the year; you avoid late filing penalties, too.

If, however, you're getting refunds — especially large refunds — you need to make adjustments so the taxes you pay throughout the year better reflect your liability. A refund is not found money. It's money you loaned to the government without earning interest on it. You wouldn't put your money in a zero-percent-interest savings account, so don't loan the government money at zero-percent interest.

You may be getting a refund because

- You haven't claimed the number of deductions to which you're entitled. Be sure to adjust your deductions as your family situation changes.
- You deliberately paid additional taxes because you expected to earn outside income from which tax deductions would not be taken, but then you didn't earn that income.

- Your employer deducted too much according to the number of dependants you're claiming, or you didn't update your deductions as your circumstances changed.

- You worked overtime. The tax table assumes you were making that income every week, resulting in too much tax being withheld.

Pay Yourself First

Paying yourself first is one of the best money management decisions you can make. Simply put, paying yourself first means you put money into a debt reduction or savings program to meet your short-term, mid-term, and long-term goals (see Chapter 5) before you pay anything else — including your rent or mortgage. If you're living from paycheque to paycheque, you may think you can't do this. But determining where you spend your money shows you how you can pay yourself first and gain many benefits.

One thing you discovered when you tracked how you spent your money in the past is that emergencies always get paid somehow. If an insurance payment came due, you skimped on restaurant meals or entertainment so you had enough money to pay that important bill before your insurance was cancelled.

If you can find the money when you absolutely must have it, you can live on less than you've been spending. The obvious conclusion is that you can put money aside for savings if you respect yourself enough to pay yourself first.

Chapter 7 goes into detail about lowering your expenses. For now, it's enough to identify the money you didn't need to spend. Put that money in the savings category of your budget. When the insurance payment came due, for example, you told yourself you didn't have money to spend on restaurant meals or movies. Isn't your future at least as important as paying for your insurance?

You'll find that when you have savings (and you will), the lowered stress, greater stability, feeling of financial security, and general well-being you enjoy are worth much more than the time and effort you invest in creating and maintaining your budget.

How to Set Up a Basic Budget

Discovering and dealing with your spending personality type give you hints on how to change your habits to create a realistic budget and keep it up to date. This section shows you how to set up a budget that reflects the reality of your current financial life.

Table 6-3 is a sample budget to show you what your budget might look like. Using the information from your spending diary, insert in the Last Month Actual column the values for what you paid in each category last month. After you determine what you should be spending in each category, put those amounts in the This Month Budget column. At the end of another month, put the amount you actually spent in each category in the This Month Actual column.

Expense	Last Month Actual	This Month Budget	This Month Actual	Over/ Under
Housing and Utilities				
Mortgage or rent				
Homeowner's or condo association fees				
Electricity				
Gas				
Water				
Telephone				
Home maintenance				
Subtotal, Housing and Utilities				
Food				
Groceries				
Restaurant meals				
Subtotal, Food				
Clothing and Shoes				

Table 6-3: *My Monthly Budget*

Expense	Last Month Actual	This Month Budget	This Month Actual	Over/ Under
Adult 1				
Adult 2				
Child 1				
Child 2				
Subtotal, Clothing and Shoes				
Insurance				
Auto				
Health				
Homeowner's/renter's				
Life				
Other				
Subtotal, Insurance				
Health Care				
Dentist				
Optometrist				
Other practitioner				
Eyeglasses, contact lenses				
Prescriptions				
Other				
Subtotal, Health Care				
Auto				
Gasoline				

(continued)

Expense	Last Month Actual	This Month Budget	This Month Actual	Over/ Under
Maintenance				
Payment				
Tolls				
Taxis and public transportation				
Subtotal, Auto				
Personal				
Charitable contributions				
Child care				
Cosmetics				
Entertainment				
Haircuts				
Magazines/newspapers				
Membership dues				
Vacations				
Other				
Subtotal, Personal				
Savings and Investments				
Savings/money market account				
Education fund				
Mutual fund				
New car fund				
New home fund				

Table 6-3: *(continued)*

Expense	Last Month Actual	This Month Budget	This Month Actual	Over/ Under
Retirement fund				
Emergency savings account				
Other				
Subtotal, Savings and Investments				
Taxes				
Federal income tax				
Provincial income tax				
CPP/EI				
Property tax				
Subtotal, Taxes				
TOTAL EXPENSES				
Income				
Gross wages 1				
Gross wages 2				
Interest income				
Alimony/child support paid to you				
Other				
TOTAL INCOME				
Difference between income and expenses (put shortages in parentheses)				

Table 6-3: *(continued)*

This budget leaves you space in the Over/Under column to compare each item's real value with its real cost. When you compile your budget, you want to be able to compare real versus projected values on a monthly, quarterly, and yearly basis.

Note that these categories are not the same as those in Table 1-2 used to calculate your debt (see Chapter 1). You'll determine which categories you need to include, but you should see how budget worksheets can vary. Choose categories that reflect your situation.

Often, your mortgage, property taxes, and insurance are lumped in one payment. Don't charge yourself twice if you pay these expenses as part of your mortgage payments.

Make sure to account for all your expenses, but put them in the category that makes your budget work for you. For example, you may want to put your homeowner's or renter's insurance under Housing and Utilities rather than under Insurance. Moving items to other categories will reflect how you spend your money; your budget will reflect how you want to allocate your resources. Also, as you recognize new items, add them to your budget.

How to Stick to Your Budget

You have many good habits that took time to cultivate. Sometimes it's hard to remember them because when you have a good habit, you don't really think about it — until you start to lose that good habit.

In the following list, check off those good habits you've already picked up:

- I pay my bills on time.
- I balance my chequebook.
- I compare prices when I shop.
- I verify the charges on my credit card statement.

None of these habits, by themselves, will make your life either wonderful or awful. But adding good habits on top of good habits improves your life immensely.

You can't just fling your old bad habits out the window. To learn to be an effective budgeter, you must coax yourself into developing good habits. Check off the following activities you can accomplish:

- Recognize how budgeting benefits me.
- Notice changes in my spending habits and decide whether the changes are good or bad.
- Revise my budget when my circumstances change.

- Seek help when I need more information.
- Set aside time every week to review my budget.
- Write down changes I want to make instead of keeping them in my head.

Failing to use and revise your budget has many drawbacks:

- You miss out on the many benefits budgeting brings to your financial life, such as the ability to make reasoned decisions rather than react to situations.
- You waste the time you already spent collecting data.
- Your stress level rises.
- You don't feel good about yourself.

How to Rein in Your Impulse Spending

You're not entirely at fault if, every time you return from the store, you have more items than you intended to purchase. Store managers have studied consumers for years. Stores purposely use floor plans that tempt you to buy things you didn't know you wanted and expose you to as many buying opportunities as possible. For example, why is milk, probably the most-purchased item in any supermarket, at the back of the store? Those wily store managers know that if you have to look at long aisles of tempting items going to and from picking up your milk, your shopping cart will likely end up with more than milk in it.

 Don't confuse good buys with impulse purchases. If you find a half-price sale on something your family uses and you can use it all before it spoils, that's a good buying decision, unless it means you can't pay another bill and will have to pay a penalty on that bill.

Common triggers

Previously, you may not have thought of your purchases as being triggered. But if the milk scenario seems familiar to you, you have your own triggers. Some common triggers follow:

- **Hunger:** You don't have the energy to make a decision, so you treat yourself to junk food rather than a nutritious meal.

- **Overwork:** You've worked hard, so you feel you deserve a treat.

- **Money in your pocket:** You have the cash to pay for it, so why not have a treat?

- **Depression:** You try to make yourself feel better by buying yourself a treat.

- **Elation:** You think nothing can go wrong when you feel so good, so you have a treat.

- **Celebration:** You or your friend/sister/brother/roommate deserves a nice present to celebrate a birthday/anniversary/new job.

- **Competition:** You have to give the nicest gift, or at least one that's as nice as so-and-so's.

- **The desire to impress someone:** You think, "Wait until so-and-so sees this!"

Ensuring your long-term financial health is the best treat you can give yourself at any time.

You probably know the kinds of things you're most likely to purchase on a whim. Go to that area of your house and write down those things you've purchased so you can see how much money you've wasted by not making thoughtful decisions.

For example, do you love buying yourself clothes? Then go to your closet. See the jacket you bought because the colour was beautiful? Of course, you have nothing that goes with it. How many items in your closet were on sale but don't really work well with the rest of your wardrobe?

Write down every item that falls into the impulse-spending category. You don't need to go through every door or find every impulse purchase, but do write down all the impulse buys you find in plain sight.

You'll use the list you make in the next section. If you're part of a couple or you're doing this exercise with your children, reassure everyone before you start this survey that its only purpose is to gather information.

If you use your survey to find fault with your or others' purchases, you'll quickly defeat the purpose and discourage helpful suggestions.

Before you go on, write an estimated cost next to each item. Then put a plus sign (+) next to anything you think you've used as much as you should have for the price. For example, you may have used your snow blower every time it snowed, but that means it has cost you $87 for each five-minute snow-removal job, so no + there! And don't forget the cost to insure that expensive piece of equipment.

Now put an asterisk (*) next to each item for which you could have purchased a reasonable substitute at a lower cost. This isn't about something that arbitrarily went on sale, but something for which a small investment of time would have resulted in paying a much lower price. Next to the asterisk, write the price you think you could have paid for a reasonable substitute. (Don't put garage-sale or second-hand-sale prices here — you have no guarantee you would have found a substitute.)

Don't ignore small impulse purchases. Although you may not have included those items in this list, you purchase them more often, so they add up quickly.

How to stop an impulse purchase

After you recognize what makes you indulge in impulse spending and what the payoff can be when you make informed purchases based on your financial goals, you can control your triggers. You can do so by making conscious decisions before the temptation to buy reaches out to grab you.

Setting your "stop" triggers doesn't mean you never get to treat yourself. If the supermarket is your downfall, for example, give yourself a set amount to spend any way you like. After a few trips to the store during which you can't decide what one treat you want, you'll find you don't want any of them all that much.

 If your impulse triggers go off in the hardware store or another type of store that sells big-ticket items, again give yourself a treat budget. If you don't have enough money to buy what you want today, you can save up your treat allowance until you have enough money in that account. But you don't get to buy now and pay with your future allowance.

Your Support Team

All kinds of people and organizations are around to help you meet your goals. In the case of people, you need to know why they want to help you, how much time and energy they can offer, and what their individual money personalities are. You may want to review the section on identifying money personalities at the end of Chapter 3 before you assign helping roles to your support team.

Spouse or significant other

The best way to work as a team with your spouse or significant other is to agree on your goals and the prioritization of those goals. You may have to compromise on individual goals to reach your goals as a couple or family.

Often, one partner is a better money manager than the other. That partner may be better at resisting temptation, computing amounts, dividing long-term goals into mid-term and short-term goals, setting priorities, balancing budgets, and so on. Or one partner may be better at some activities while the other is better at the remaining tasks.

The secret to a good partnership is jointly agreeing to goals and how you're going to reach those goals. Then each partner does the best job possible for his or her responsibilities. In spite of the word *partner,* you may decide to give one person more authority than the other — as long as you both agree on who should have more authority when it comes to financial matters, and remember that financial security, not being in charge, is your goal. As time goes on and changes need to be made, use the same negotiating and compromising that brought you as far as you are to help you set up a new system.

Children

If you have children, you certainly want to involve them in learning how to handle money. Keeping children involved in the budgeting process also helps them learn the financial lessons they need to know at each stage in their lives.

For example, when your children start getting allowances, you might want to deduct 10 percent from each child's allowance. Needless to say, the first few deductions will cause much upset. The lesson is that adults don't get to keep all they earn because they must pay taxes. Just as adults get police and fire protection and roads to drive on from their taxes, the children get a place to live, meals, and vacations from their "taxes."

Or if your children's dog gets sick, perhaps have them use part of their savings to help pay the veterinarian's bill. They will learn what savings are for and how they can meet goals by saving today.

No child is too young to participate in the family budget. But the younger a child is, the shorter term the goal must be to fit with young children's shortened attention span and patience. If your children are not part of your "budgeting board of directors," everyone gets cheated. They not only miss out on important lessons, but their feelings and wishes are not reflected in two strategic parts of family life: budgeting and buying decisions.

Parents

Your parents have lived longer and met and survived more financial challenges than you have. Their individual and collective money personalities are important as to what kinds of help they can provide and what kinds of help you want from them.

If your parents can handle requests for loans and advice in a businesslike manner (and if you'll respond with an equally businesslike attitude), you can ask for loans and advice. If they have the attitude that whoever pays gets to make the rules, they'll probably want more control and expect answers to more questions than you're willing to give them. If you're desperate for their help, you may have to live with their money personalities. However, try to avoid asking parents for money because it can lead to family strife down the road.

Friends

Friends have many of the same pluses and minuses that parents do, except you aren't required to keep them forever. One of the benefits of friends' involvement in helping you reach your goals is that you can restrict them to just one area of your financial decision making.

You may think you know your friends well, but personalities can clash when money enters the picture. If a friend gives you a loan, draw up a written agreement on the amount of the loan, when it is to be repaid, and how much interest is to be paid. If your friend suddenly decides the loan gives permission to tell you how to run your business or your life or your child's life, diplomatically remind your friend of the contract.

Still, you may identify friends from whom you'd like advice on your finances. You can invite those friends into your financial circle based on your ability to work with the strengths and weaknesses of each person's money personality. If someone is a closer friend to one marriage partner than the other, the two of you must discuss and negotiate that factor as well. As you set financial priorities, your good relations with your partner must take precedence over getting advice or help from a friend.

Professional and free services

Professional sources can help you gather information, set goals, set priorities, or stay on your financial path. You can use these sources from the start, use them once in a while, or even discard them from your financial life when their purpose has been served.

Accountants do much more than fill out tax returns. They can help you set goals, remind you of factors you have forgotten or ignored, use their backgrounds with a variety of people's problems and solutions, start you on a good financial plan no matter what your age or income, help you revise your plans and goals as you get older, and — the part you'll probably enjoy the most — help you reduce the taxes you pay.

Depending on your accountant's practice, you may also be able to get information about estate planning, insurance practices, housing, health care, and scholarships.

Your employer, union, or trade organization may have an EAP (employee assistance program). The services an EAP offers vary from provider to provider. Although some services may not be strictly financial, getting free or low-cost services in any area of concern will positively affect your financial situation and your ability to reach your goals.

Some EAPs offer budgeting, savings, tax, and estate planning services, either individually or in groups. The programs may also offer substance abuse help, family or individual counselling, workshops on buying and maintaining a home, and credit counselling. Whatever the topic, if you need information about it and don't pay for it, you've eliminated that budget expense while still learning what you need to know.

Your house of worship, community groups, credit bureaus, libraries, schools, financial institutions, and associations may offer budgeting and savings programs, either free or at a low cost. Look in local newspapers and newsletters for ads announcing such programs. Your local library or social service agency may also keep track of such listings.

How to Deal with Emergency Expenses

Unexpected expenses can severely disrupt your financial status. The four situations that usually get people in financial trouble are as follows:

- Health care emergencies
- Vehicle repair and replacement
- Expensive appliances that wear out
- Helping family or friends with their money troubles

Those expenses are the reason you have an emergency expense fund. If your fund isn't large enough, however, you can take short-term actions to avoid ending up in a spiral of debt:

- If your income is low, ask a local government or social services agency if low- or no-interest loans are available for these types of emergencies. Religious organizations also may have such funds.

- Ask your credit card companies and other creditors to let you skip a payment without penalty. They'll still add an interest charge, which raises your total debt, but the tactic frees up immediate money so you can take care of the emergency.

- Pawn some possessions. Pawning is really a secured loan — you get cash in exchange for an item of value. If you pay back the loan (with interest, of course) by the deadline, you can retrieve your item.

- If you have a medical emergency, ask your health care provider about available services that would offset expenses for you, such as free or low-cost housing while your loved one is in the hospital and free or low-cost meals.

- If your problem is with your car and you have a good relationship with a garage, try to negotiate a time-payment plan at low or no interest (rather than the higher rate you would be paying on your credit card).

- Take out a home-equity loan or second mortgage. These are not the best choices, however, because the exposure to upward interest rate changes tends to be very high. And be sure to read the fine print. On some of those loans, you could lose your house if you miss one loan payment. Make sure, too, that you have the right to pay off the loan early to reduce the interest expense.

- If you belong to a social or service organization, find out whether it has a formal or informal system for help-ing members. For example, a student from Norway who came to study in Canada discovered that because of a miscommunication, he had arrived two weeks before his housing was available. He was a member of

Mensa, so he called the local contact. Someone in the local group put him up, rent free, for the two weeks — and gave him a tour of the local area, topped off with a Labour Day picnic.

Be creative. This is another situation in which knowing the financial (and other) personalities of your family members and friends helps. The boldest family member or friend, or the one with the strongest saver personality, will be the best negotiator for these perks.

Paying for an emergency by credit card may get you in debt at a high interest rate (in the high teens). If you must use a credit card, be sure to choose the one with the lowest interest rate (probably in the low teens). Now may be the time to take advantage of one of those low-introductory-rate cards a lender has offered to you — but do so only if you can pay off the balance before the introductory rate expires or if the regular rate is reasonable.

Record Organization

Your role as a money manager won't seem so burdensome if you know you have what you need to succeed. Why begin a weekly or monthly money management session with a sense of frustration because you can't find the information you want or need? Make it easy for yourself and use the information in this chapter to support your money managing efforts.

Getting organized is at least half the battle in developing money management skills. If you just take the time, purchase a few supplies, and follow the simple steps identified in this section, you're well on your way as a successful money manager. Make an appointment to meet with yourself every week — a short half-hour meeting will do. Then move into a monthly appointment where you allow an hour.

Getting started really doesn't take much. You need the following supplies to organize your financial records. If you don't have them, make a shopping list and go to the store:

- **Pens, pencils, paper, paper clips, and manila folders:** Tabbed folders let you see your records at a glance.

- **A file container:** You can use a cardboard box, a plastic crate, or a regular filing cabinet — whatever matches your budget.

- **Envelopes and postage stamps:** A box of business envelopes makes your financial correspondence and payments easier. Have a supply of stamps on hand, too, so you can be sure to make your payments on time.

- **An appointment book, a notebook, or a digital device:** Record your business appointments and any expenditures you can't track with receipts.

• **Software:** Add-on software programs (those that may not come with the computer) such as Quicken and Microsoft Money can help you organize and track financial information.

After you start the process of organizing your financial records, you want to stay on track. Visit your folders often, update your financial information regularly, and maybe even schedule a monthly appointment with yourself to help you stay organized.

Folders for keeping your financial records

Label a folder (include the year on the label) for each of the following items that applies to your financial situation. Put your folders in alphabetical order in your file container. Add additional folders as your situation calls for them.

• Automobile — Insurance and loan
• Automobile — Maintenance
• Bank accounts
• Charitable contributions
• Credit cards
• Educational records, tuition receipts
• Health insurance
• Home — Improvements

- Home — Insurance
- Home — Maintenance
- Home — Mortgage
- Income tax — Federal
- Income tax — Provincial
- Insurance — Life and disability
- Loan (specify type)
- Mutual funds
- Property tax bills
- Real estate investment
- Registered education savings plan (RESP)
- Registered retirement savings plan (RRSP)
- Tax-free savings accounts (TFSA)
- Investments in shares
- Travel, passport, frequent flyer plans
- Warranties
- Will or trust or both

Consolidate all the information you have and add it to each folder pertaining to that file. Record essential information on the cover of each folder. Identify the name, address, phone number, and number for each account, policy, or whatever. Collecting this information takes a little time but makes contacts and record keeping much easier during the year. Table 6-4 shows an example of what you may need for your insurance file. Fill in the information and staple it to the inside cover of the relevant folder. Some forms can do double duty.

Insurance (automobile, health, home, life, and disability)	
Insurance company/financial institution	
Address	
Phone	
Name of representative	
Phone, if different from above	
Claim number	
Policy number	
Payments	
Other	
Communication log	
Date, name, results	
Date, name, results	
Date, name, results	

Table 6-4: *Tracking Insurance*

These basic forms illustrate the kind of essential information needed for each of your folders. When you have information at your fingertips, you put it to better and more frequent use.

Personal records

You'll also benefit from keeping personal information in one place. So while you're organizing, set up a personal file with the following information:

- **Social insurance number(s):** Include your social insurance number, as well as those of your spouse, your children, your parents, and your siblings.

- **Contact information:** List the names and addresses of each of your adult children and your parents. Include work-contact information when available.

- **Passports and birth certificates:** Collect the original documents for each member of your family and keep them in this folder.

- **Marriage certificate/divorce decree:** Include your marriage certificate or divorce documents or both in your folder.

- **Personal will:** No matter what your age, make sure you have an up-to-date will. If you already have a will, take another look at it to see whether you need to make adjustments. If you don't have a will, make getting one a priority.

- **Living will:** You can ask your doctor to draw up a statement for a living will, or pick up a form to fill out. Share this information with your family and keep a copy in your personal folder.

7

Spending Wisely

Reducing your expenses may sound like a negative experience. Think of all the things you'd have to do without! When you pare your expenses, however, you feel the delight of having your spending under control. A bonus is the disappearance of the stress of not knowing how you're going to pay your bills and plan for your future. When you make spending decisions before you even leave your home, and you know sticking to those decisions will help you meet your goals, you won't spend time and energy on every spending decision.

If your best planning still finds "more month than money," the solution is to increase your income. Like you never thought of that, right? The difference is that in the past, your plan consisted of dreaming "if only I made more money."

In this chapter, you explore how to determine the amount you need, how to figure out whether your need is short-term or long-term, and how to know exactly where you can find your personal pot of gold.

Alternatives to Spending

Chapter 3 suggests ways to monitor your spending, such as using various coloured highlighters to categorize your purchases as they appear on your bank and credit card statements, or using computer software to track your finances. No matter your method, categorize your spending so you can create your own wise spending pattern.

As you categorize your spending, you can change your categories or add and subtract categories. One important note to keep in mind is that your system shouldn't frustrate you to the point where you stop your efforts to control your spending. Your financial health is important, so make your system easy to follow and to stick to.

Spend, rent, or borrow?

When the lawn is as high as an elephant's eye, do you go out and buy a lawn mower? Doing so would seem logical . . . except that your lawn takes only half an hour to mow. Once a week. Maximum.

Does your neighbour have the hugest, most magnificent maple tree in the province — with piles of autumn leaves in the yard to go with it? Raking all those leaves is a big job — for 1 month out of 12. Is that month of activity worth purchasing a leaf blower?

Make a list of everything you own. Expand the list by adding things you forgot the first time around, and then writing down what each item cost and how often you use it. (And check out Chapter 4 for more about distinguishing between needs and wants.) Until you decided to get control of your spending, you probably thought you needed each of these things because you use them. Listing how much they cost and how often you use them gives you a new perspective.

Note that the cost of insuring, maintaining, and storing rarely used items is an ongoing expense, even for appliances that are paid for. Make sure to factor these costs into your list.

For each item you own but rarely use, you have four choices:

- Keep it and use it until it wears out.

- Sell the item and then rent or borrow a replacement only when you have a need for it.

- Sell the item and then pay someone to perform that chore with his or her own equipment.

- Find a lower-cost alternative to the item.

After you pick one of these four choices, put a new cost on each item in your list. How much money could you free up by renting, borrowing, or co-owning?

After you have this information, how will you use it? The choices you have tell you not only what to do with your current appliances but also how to handle future needs. For example, when the leaf blower can't huff and puff anymore, you have four choices:

- Replace it.
- Rent a leaf blower only when the leaves come a-tumbling down.
- Make arrangements to borrow someone else's leaf blower when the need arises.
- Use a rake.

 Whether you're renting, borrowing, or co-owning, make sure your partners share your attitude on maintenance, cleanup, storage, and general care of tools and appliances.

Spend or barter?

With the proper incentive, anyone can make a deal. You may say you don't know how to barter, but return for a minute to your childhood and you'll see you've always had the skill. Remember the words, "But Mom, if you buy me this toy, I'll eat all my vegetables for a week"?

Even in the grown-up world, you have negotiating skills —
and bartering is negotiating. Maybe you want your washing machine fixed, your lawn mowed, or your eavestroughs
cleaned out. All you need to do is find something you can do
for someone else in return for the service you need. For example, you help a friend with his résumé and, in exchange, he
helps build you some bookshelves.

You have skills to trade, too. Think about the things you
can do that other people want done for them. Make a list of
all the skills you use at work or in pursuing your hobbies —
designing websites, filling out tax returns, hanging wallpaper,
taking photographs, and so on. Note that personal skills (for
example, closet reorganizing) and thinking skills (for example,
planning a vacation) are tradable, too.

Using a fresh piece of paper (or a new computer file), start
a list of all your skills. Keep this list with you. As you go about
your life, you'll think of more and more skills to add to this list.
You may want to divide the list into things you're willing to
do, things you'll do if you have to, and things you don't ever
want to do again.

Consider bartering clubs, which may facilitate this
part of your money management. To find a bartering
club, look in your local Yellow Pages, search the
Internet, ask a librarian, or check with neighbourhood
organizations, professional and trade associations,
service organizations, alumni associations, and houses
of worship.

Every club has its own rules, but like any other organization, someone has to pay the organization's costs, such as accounting costs, mail costs, and promotion fees. If you're interested in joining a bartering club, you need to know the following information:

- Is there a fee to join? Is it an annual fee?
- What fees are assessed on barters?
- Who belongs now? (Get a list.)
- Are the club membership and services growing or shrinking?
- How long has the club been in existence?
- Can you drop your membership whenever you want, as long as you "pay" whatever outstanding "debt" is in your account?

 Find out as much as you can about a club before you join. If other members aren't reliable, are so fussy they'll always complain about your contribution, or live so far away they can't fulfill your needs, don't join.

Your Lifestyle Makeover

Giving your lifestyle a makeover is not the same as lowering your standard of living or depriving yourself. In fact, it can be the opposite. The emphasis here is on style. As the preceding sections on sharing and bartering demonstrate, a lifestyle makeover involves an attitude shift that will help you get the most for your dollar. The following sections can help you reach your financial goals.

Use coupons rather than pay full price

The art of saving money by using coupons is a consumer industry in itself. Whether you've never used coupons or you use them and want to get more from your efforts, the tips in this section can help you meet your goals.

Couponing is a skill for which reading carefully pays off. First, you have to find coupons. Check newspapers and newspaper inserts, the packaging of items you've already bought, the back of your supermarket receipts, and coupon trade boxes inside stores, to name a few sources. Before buying a product you know you want, check out company websites for coupons and other promotional items. This approach works especially well for food and pharmaceutical items.

 Don't buy something just because you have a coupon for it. If you won't use the product for a while, you have to store it; if it's something you don't like, you'll never use it.

Keep up with the Joneses, but get better deals

Membership warehouse clubs, such as Costco or Sam's Club Canada, can come to your aid with special deals. Because these organizations buy in bulk, they often get a lower rate and can pass those savings along to you.

 If you're planning a car trip and a gasoline credit card offers hotel discounts, this may be the time to obtain that card. If you have trouble with overspending on credit cards, close out your account as soon as the trip is over.

Keep in mind that you don't have to spend a lot to have fun

 When you first determined to get your financial house in order, you probably thought entertainment was going to go by the wayside. Even with cable, television is a poor long-term amusement. Luckily, you have many other options:

- **Support — and enjoy — the arts.** If the theatre, the opera, and live music are your passion, you can enjoy them without breaking your budget. Many performances offer discounted rush seats on the day of the show.

- **Cruise for deals.** Some travel agencies sell off cruises and other deals at good prices to people who can fill vacancies at the last minute. You can buy into these deals at 50 percent or less of the listed price. Sometimes you have to become a member of a travel group's club to be notified of an opening. Will you use or save enough to make membership fees worthwhile? These discounted offers are great, especially for retirees and self-employed people, whose schedules are more flexible.

- **Browse for can't-beat airfare.** Nearly all the major airlines offer last-minute airfare deals that allow you to take off on spur-of-the-moment weekend trips. You have to sign up to receive these email updates, and they often include special rates on car rentals and hotel rates in the destinations to which the special fares apply. Check out individual airline websites, or go to www.travelzoo.com/ca/, an online discount travel site that does trip searching and helps you book trips, too. Travelzoo's offerings cater to last-minute deals and sell-offs.

Spend less and enjoy life more

Look for your own opportunities to reduce your expenses without reducing your quality of life. Instead of always looking to your wallet to pay for entertainment, use the creative skills you've been developing. Knowledgeable, reliable people are in demand everywhere. Consider the following examples:

- Does your child's class need a chaperone for a school trip? Volunteer for the job.
- If you can't devote the time to be a regular usher at a theatre, offer a skill or time in trade for attending a dress rehearsal.
- If you like sports, find out what personnel are needed to put on an event. Could you be an assistant coach for a children's soccer or baseball league? Can you help organize a local tennis tournament?
- Can you speak a second language? Offer a friend language lessons in exchange for her teaching you to play guitar.

How to Live on Less

If you went to the store to buy one size and brand of bread and could pay either $2.00 or $2.50 for it, which would you choose? Sounds like a dumb question, doesn't it? Yet every day, people make the wrong decision.

 Here are some ways to live on less without sacrificing quality of life:

- **Dig for deep discounts.** Shop at very-deep-discount stores instead of convenience stores, and buy the same items for less. Browse the Internet for a local or area-wide directory of discount and outlet stores.

- **Brown-bag it.** Take your lunch to work instead of buying it; you'll have a healthier lunch and save money, too.

- **Telecommute, if you can.** Negotiate with your employer to work at home. You can save restaurant, travel, car wear and tear, and clothing expenses.

 Negotiate who is going to pay for equipment, telephone lines, and other expenses. If those expenses are your responsibility, you may be spending instead of saving money.

- **Analyze your purchase decisions.** Understand your real goal before you make a purchase. If you want to lose weight, you can do so for free by walking in the park or by taking advantage of the company gym. Either one is cheaper than signing a contract at an exercise facility.

- **Consider the previously owned.** A used car is new to you. Not only do you pay less, but your insurance costs are less than on a new car, your depreciation is slower, and you don't have to dread that first ding in the door.

- **Always use a shopping list.** Just as the lines on the highway keep you driving in the lane, a shopping list keeps you from giving in to temptation. Even if you decide to purchase something not on your list, you will have considered and weighed the purchase.

What to Do with Your Found Money

The fastest way to undo all your hard work is to think of your money as a tradeoff between spending on one item and spending on another. Yes, you can take advantage of the savings that come from buying in quantity — if you've figured in waste, storage costs, and the other possible expenses of having a large quantity of one item on hand.

If you release yourself from always worrying about money by reducing your expenses, you may feel rich because you at last have cash in your pocket. That found money should go first toward debt reduction (as Chapter 2 discusses in depth) and then toward savings.

Does paying off debts and then putting money toward savings mean you don't get to enjoy the fruits of your labour? Of course not. You get to enjoy being free from worry, seeing your debts disappear, and watching your savings grow.

While you're paying off debts and starting a savings program with your found money, don't even think about the credit available on your credit cards. Using that credit means more debt, which is exactly what you don't want.

How to Earn Additional Income

If all your money-saving, coupon-cutting, and planning still leave you short of achieving your goals, look for ways to earn more income:

- **Get a raise — yes, it's possible!** Contact trade associations, your alumni association, and unions, and do research at the library or on the Internet to find out what others doing your job are earning. If you find your wage is lower than average, take your research to your boss and ask for a raise.

- **Take an inventory of your skills.** Look for skills you use at work but maybe aren't appreciated by your boss and aren't being recognized in your paycheque. Bosses don't have to think about what's going right — so they don't! You need to remind your boss about your accomplishments. If you can prove you're underpaid, negotiate a raise.

- **Allow your hobbies to earn you extra money.** For example, if you know how to work with wood, you can sell the furniture you build or help people build things for a fee. You may have to do a little research to see how much you should charge customers, but hobbies still are a good source of income that's a pleasure to earn.

Not only do you need to survey your knowledge and skills to see where you might earn extra income, but you also must decide how much you want to earn and what it will cost you to do so. Be sure to calculate material and tool expenditures as well as time expenditures. Will you recoup your investment? Will you have enough income to write off those expenditures on your income taxes as business expenses?

Think about whether you want to take on any extra work for a short, medium, or long period of time:

- **Short-term need:** If you want to do extra work only long enough to pay off your credit card or other debt, you may want to look for seasonal work or register with a temporary-employment agency. Because you won't be working extra for a long time (you get to define *long*), you'll probably have the energy to work longer hours, work more days per week, commute a little farther, and so on.

- **Mid-term need:** If this extra job is going to go on for a while because you need the extra income for a longer period, such as while your child grows up, you don't want to commit yourself to so many hours, so much travel, or so many days per week that you don't have a life. That's a quick way to burn out. Not only will you fail to reach your goals, you'll be discouraged and may even think you can't reach your goals or that budgeting doesn't work.

- **Long-term need:** To earn extra income for a long-term need, such as retirement, consider the same things you did for a mid-term need. Recognize that the decisions you make will affect your lifestyle for a long time.

If you're going to be forced to spend more time at work, have more commuting costs, or have wasted dead time (blocks of time between jobs that are long enough to be annoying but short enough that you can't use them for naps, grocery shopping, or whatever), it may be time to consider cutting back on your lifestyle. Moving to less expensive housing, sharing housing, seeking sales, bartering more aggressively, and so on will allow you to make more life-enhancing decisions sooner.

For mid-term or long-term extra income needs, consider trading some of the income for cutting back on your lifestyle. The tips in this chapter can help you make your money go further so you can enjoy your life and still get out of debt and start a savings program.

About the Authors

Andrew Dagys, CPA, CMA, is a best-selling author who has written and co-authored more than a dozen books, mostly about investing, personal finance, and technology. Andrew has contributed columns to major Canadian publications. He is also a frequently quoted author in many of Canada's daily news publications, including *The Globe and Mail, National Post* and *Toronto Star.* He has appeared on several national news broadcasts to offer his insights on the Canadian and global investment landscapes. Andrew considers writing books, in collaboration with talented publishing and editorial partners, to be one of life's most truly amazing experiences.

Andrew enjoys actively serving his community in the not-for-profit sector. He lives in Toronto with his wife, Dawn-Ava, and their three children — Brendan, Megan, and Jordan.

Mary Reed is a personal finance writer who has coauthored and written numerous books on topics related to consumer money matters and legal rights.

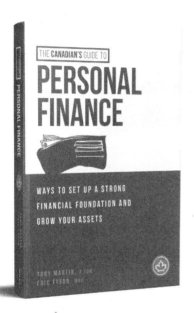
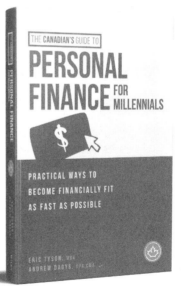

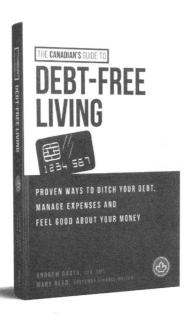

978-1-119-60933-9

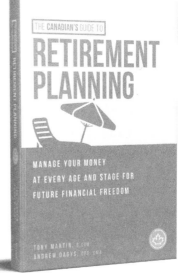

978-1-119-60996-4

THE CANADIAN'S GUIDE TO

STARTING A SMALL BUSINESS

OPEN

SMART CONSIDERATIONS
AND STRAIGHT FORWARD STEPS TO
LAUNCH YOUR BUSINESS IDEA

ANDREW DABYS, CPA, CGA
MARGARET KERNS
JOANNE KERTZ

978-1-119-60926-1

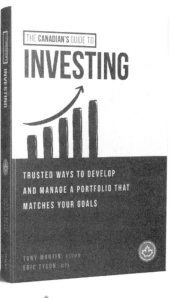

THE CANADIAN'S GUIDE TO

INVESTING

TRUSTED WAYS TO DEVELOP
AND MANAGE A PORTFOLIO THAT
MATCHES YOUR GOALS

TONY MARTIN, BCOMM
ERIC TYSON, MBA

978-1-119-60995-7

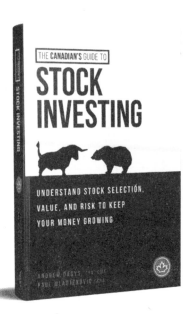

THE CANADIAN'S GUIDE TO
STOCK INVESTING

UNDERSTAND STOCK SELECTION,
VALUE, AND RISK TO KEEP
YOUR MONEY GROWING

ANDREW DAGYS, CPA, CMA
PAUL MLADJENOVIC, CFP

978-1-119-61189-9

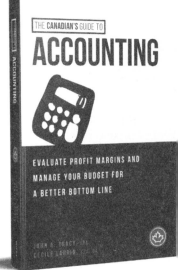

THE CANADIAN'S GUIDE TO
ACCOUNTING

EVALUATE PROFIT MARGINS AND
MANAGE YOUR BUDGET FOR
A BETTER BOTTOM LINE

JOHN A. TRACY, CPA
CECILE LAURIN, CPA, CA

978-1-119-60934-6